Small Farm Leadership

Grow yourself.

Grow People, Products, and Profits

Jason McClure

A Grow Your Own Way Publication

Printed in the United States of America

First Printing, 2019

ISBN: 9798646101076

Grow Your Own Books and Courses

1278 Mill Creek Circle

Salem, AR 72576

GrowYourOwnWayBooks.com

"Let us not forget that the cultivation of the Earth is the most important labor of man. When tillage begins, other arts will follow. The farmers, therefore, are the founders of civilization."

~ Daniel Webster

Contents

About this book 5

Grow a Leadership Foundation 8

Grow a Farm Leader's Mindset..13

    Leadership thinking 13
    Dare to dream 15
    Be visionary..17
    Leadership is a process...18
    People follow purpose..21
    7 Effective farm leader types..22

Grow Enduring Traditions 26

    Philosophical traditions of small farmers 32
    Tradition of enlightenment..32
    Tradition of education..35
    Tradition of evolution..42
    Tradition of effort 45
    Tradition of engagement...50
    Managing traditions 54

Grow Self-Investment 60

    Investing in competence...60
    Investing in self-efficacy 62
    Investing in character 69
    Investing in appreciation...74
    Investing in motivation 78
    Investing in commitment 82
    Investing in self-discipline 85

Grow a Farm Visionary Mindset...87

    Others don't do it this way 87
    Farm vision development 91
    Mission development..93
    Think big, start small..95
    Innovation 97

Intentional focus 99
Fail forward...101
Growing People, Growing Farms 103
Hiring right 105
Training 110
Coaching...115
Mentoring..118
Providing feedback..123
Terminating employees....................................126
Grow Community 131
Organizational culture 133
Building strong culture 138
Develop a loyal following 141
Grow a Farm Legacy 146
Why do you farm? 146
Create something that matters........................147
22 Leadership Principles 149
Useful Quotes 151

About this book

This book is for small farmers with big dreams. I believe small farms, homesteads, and urban gardens are bonafide businesses that should provide owners with a substantial profit. Too many people pursue these endeavors as nothing more than a side hustle, an extra money maker, or a hobby. This book is not for those people.

This book is for people who believe small farm or urban garden activities are important entrepreneurial activities pursued with passion, purpose, and pride. The goal of this book is to provide leadership insights and skills necessary to build a sustainable business. This book is a farm leadership book, not a farm management book. Farm management books focus on raising produce or animals, soil management, or operations, whereas this book focuses on developing people.

More specifically, this book focuses on leadership development on the individual level, given the small farm context. Leadership is more than a position; it is a way of thinking, being, and interacting with others.

Leaders don't follow. Ralph Waldo Emerson said it this way, "*Do not go where the path may lead, go instead where there is no path and leave a trail.*" Many farmers follow the same paths toward mediocrity, status quo maintenance, and bankruptcy. Not enough farmers create their paths toward achievement, progress, and prosperity.

I have read many business books, including farm business books. I discovered a lack of leadership material developed and directed toward small or family farms, rural America, and urban market gardeners. Most farm business resources ignore or barely discuss visionary leadership, organizational culture, and growing people. Currently, when searching "farm leadership" on Amazon, nothing much appears.

This lack of resources is both unfortunate and appalling. Small farms are bonafide businesses; however, publishers, authors, and consultants routinely overlook this essential industry. These people underestimate the power of small farms, rural economic development, and the American Dream.

Leadership development, strategic management, and organizational development industries focus on big business and mega-corporations; visiting any bookstore or website verifies this. You will discover thousands of titles by "experts" who boast about their importance to the Fortune 500. What you will not see are experts boasting about their dedication to small farms.

Small farms are important economic engines that play an essential role in rural economic development. These farms deserve the same recognition, attention, and societal appreciation other businesses enjoy. Lastly, a small farm is an opportunity to live the American Dream: your farm dream.

This book is on a mission to provide small farmers with the same body of knowledge that large businesses use to compete against small farms. Mega-corporations want nothing more than to rule the world. If you do not believe this, keep in mind that **69 of the top 100 world economies are corporations**. Recently, Apple's market value reached one trillion dollars!

It is a mistake to think these companies are satisfied with their obscene earnings and massive size. They are not. They want to grow, reduce costs, and make even more money. These corporations have a single goal: profit maximization.

Competition from corporations hurts small family farms. For example, Wal-Mart is buying and consolidating dairies. Costco is investing in chicken houses. Tyson owns all the inputs from a chicken's hatching to the final processing.

These companies use the process known as vertical integration (owning and controlling more production methods) to earn more profits. These actions are why fewer dairy farms, independent chicken farmers, and family farms exist. The result is more economic unrest for rural America. This book will give you an edge and help small farmers to compete with big corporations. This book will keep your farm growing your way.

Grow a Leadership Foundation

"Management is doing things right; leadership is doing the right things." ~ Peter F. Drucker

You are a farm leader; therefore, you are accountable for all successes and failures on the journey to sustainable farming. All farmers do two things: grow and build. Small farm leaders understand this applies to people as well as products and infrastructure.

Small farm leaders understand small farm building is actually business building, and any building requires a solid foundation. The small farm foundation is purpose, product, and people.

- **Purpose.** People desire a purpose beyond a paycheck. All people need accomplishment and a place to belong and contribute. Effective leadership builds a workplace of belonging, creating, and contribution — a workplace that provides meaning.

  This need for contribution is the primary reason people volunteer with non-profits or religious organizations. This volunteer work provides people with a sense of purpose and belonging, something lacking in most workplaces.

  Small farms are the perfect places to give people purpose and a community: a place to belong. This connection is a byproduct of a farm vision higher than growing vegetables or raising animals.

  Farming without vision and purpose is just a series of tasks that "pays the bills." With imagination and a mission in mind, farming is elevated to a calling: a pursuit bringing meaning and joy to life.

Purpose cultivates significance. Pursuing big goals inspires action, and big dreams come from a definite purpose. Lofty small farm goals can include saving the environment, providing healthy food, eliminating feedlots, and various other ideals. Whatever purpose, ideal, or pursuit a small farm leader pursues, it becomes a life guided by a mission, passion, and accomplishment.

- **Products**. For small farms to stay in business, they must sell something profitable. Farm managers raise and sell commodities; whereas, farm leaders develop and promote attractive, innovative, and branded value-added products.

  Product development must be customer-centered. In short, people must want what you are selling. The food market is competitive. Expecting people to buy your farm products because you grew something is unrealistic.

- **People**. People are why small farms thrive. People make decisions, complete tasks, and buy products. Without people, we do not need farms. The idea that people need to thank a farmer for eating is misguided. If you farm, you should be thanking people for allowing you to farm.

  People inside organizations complete tasks. Good employees require a fair (market-appropriate) wage, decent working conditions, and professional development. Too many employers limit the discussion of working conditions to the physical environment while not understanding it includes people's treatment.

Treating all people well is not only good business; it is the right thing to do. Treating employees or associates well creates a happy productive workforce. Treating customers well establishes a loyal customer base. Remember, while customers must eat, **they do not have to eat your food**. Leaders understand customer-centered businesses thrive in markets where other companies fail.

Dependable people working with purpose while delivering quality products build sustainable businesses. You have a dream of turning a farm into a viable business. It makes you different from most other small farmers. The fact is too many small farms or homesteads view their operation as just mere "side hustles" or hobbies. As a result of the owners' limited thinking, they rob themselves of an abundant future, limit local economic development, and prevent customers from enjoying locally grown products.

The primary difference between struggling farms and thriving farms is how owners think. Any farm can grow into something bigger and better when owners shift their thinking. The key to success in any industry — especially in a highly competitive, regulated, and declining industry such as farming — is leadership. Most farmers are great managers, yet they struggle. Visionary leadership transforms struggling farmers into thriving farmers.

If a person can read, they can lead. Reading this book and others like it is leadership development. All successful small businesses, including small farms, depend on people to carry out the work. For this reason alone, growing people is essential for any business, including small farming.

Growing people who can tackle most of the daily and routine farm tasks is freeing. Competent and capable people allow leaders to do more marketing, relationship building, planning, and a host of other business growth activities. The more refined a person's leadership becomes, the more effectively a person can lead others.

Effective small farm leadership builds a culture and empowers people. When this happens, leaders have more personal and professional freedom. This freedom comes from being able to delegate tasks to competent capable people who can problem-solve.

Many people want to be wealthy. There is nothing wrong with that goal; however, one person cannot single-handedly work enough hours to become wealthy as a small farmer. Many people want the freedom to schedule their work; however, schedule flexibility is a mere pipe dream without dependable people.

This chapter opened with a quote from Peter Drucker, stating leadership is about doing the right things. Building a farm that serves as a source of life lessons is the right thing to do. A shared dream among many small farmers is to leave their farms to their heirs. A more significant legacy is for their heirs to embrace their predecessors' motivation, reasons, and enthusiasm for farming in a way that allows the heirs to pursue dreams of their own design.

Sharing these reasons with children and grandchildren create life lessons that will sustain offspring no matter what occupations or paths they pursue. Passing on knowledge, passion, and purpose is the best way to ensure you have positively impacted their lives long after you are gone.

I farm because I want my children to know that hard work, innovation, dedication, integrity, and family are essential success principles. I also want my children and, eventually, their children and grandchildren to have a special place to call home. Regardless of how spread out they become, I'm creating a place of refuge, restoration, and revival for future generations.

Small farmers must adopt a leadership mindset. Anything less is a disservice to themselves, family, and community. I say this because as America grew, farming provided the first means of production and prosperity, laying the foundation for the nation's expansion.

Leaders, not managers, will solve many of the problems facing small or family farms. Management is a position limited in scope and creativity; whereas, leadership is more than a position. It is a purposeful person living with hope and passion.

Purpose comes alive when expressed as a dream. Effective small farm leaders are dreamers with the gumption to make things happen where other people fail. Gumption brings with it courage, persistence, and confidence. People with gumption stand behind their convictions, know what they are doing and why. People with gumption are leaders.

Grow a Farm Leader's Mindset

"Becoming a leader is synonymous with becoming yourself. It is precisely that simple, and it is also that difficult."
~ **Warren Bennis**

Leadership begins within. It is an intrinsic desire to achieve substantial personal growth, accomplish lofty goals, and create corporate greatness. This book takes an inside-out leadership approach by building on the principle that all great accomplishments start with an individual committed to a lofty aspiration.

The most basic intrinsic activity is thinking. What and how people think determines their mindsets. We all have perspectives, but these mindsets are not always actively or adequately managed. Leaders think differently, which is why they act differently. It is much more than a cliché to say, *"to change your life, change your thoughts."* This statement is a core axiom of leadership, motivational thought, and personal development; it is the definitive success principle.

Leadership thinking

"A man who does not think for himself does not think at all."
~ **Oscar Wilde**

The need for small farm leadership in rural America is at an all-time high. Rural America has been economically declining my entire life, and the U.S. Department of Agriculture's Economic Research Service confirms this. According to their research, rural communities have been losing population for decades, a trend with no sign of reversal.

As a child, I remember adults telling me that there was no future on the farms around Pine Snag, Arkansas. These well-meaning people said to me if I wanted to make money, I must leave. To an extent, they were right, but they were also wrong.

They were wrong because opportunity existed. It still exists. The problem was (and still is) they did not see it for me because they did not see it for themselves. They were right in that there were no major employers or industries in the area. Yes, these things provide jobs, security, and opportunity, but no industry or employer holds a monopoly on prosperity.

This collective mindset created a local leadership void. This situation is not limited to the Pine Snag of the past but continues in the present. It sadly includes thousands of rural communities across America. V.S. Naipaul says it this way, "*Most people are not really free. They are confined by the niche in the world that they carve out for themselves. They limit themselves to fewer possibilities by the narrowness of their vision.*"

Here is a fact. Urban areas were not always massive metropolitan areas, and none of today's global businesses started as large businesses. All large communities or businesses started small. Also, urban areas grew as people within those areas built and developed industry. The builders of economies have always been and will always be visionaries.

Rural economic development only happens with local leadership. The change needed to improve local economies will emerge from private citizens, not from any level of government, local chambers of commerce, or local education providers. This change will start with an individual dreamer who will be chastised, ridiculed, and mocked by poor people who are poor in the worst way – poor in dreams. **The dreamers will unleash rural America's economic power.**

Dare to dream

> *"Every great dream begins with a dreamer."*
> **~Harriet Tubman**

Dreams are the ultimate economic engine. Politicians and community leaders love to talk big and promise people the moon and sky. These people tout tax incentives and the importance of developing the *"workforce of tomorrow."* Their hollow promises do not attract industry or spur economic development, let alone create meaningful long-term results.

Whether it be a region, county, or town, virtually all small communities have a mostly empty industrial tech park — one that when built promised prosperity. Today, these industrial parks are giving way to empty high-tech parks. Just as the industrial parks have been vacant for decades, many of these new high-tech parks are going to sit empty.

I am no cynic, and this book is proof of that. If anything, I am too much of an idealistic dreamer; however, I understand principles guide reality. I also understand that my success is my responsibility. Personal accountability, initiative, and creativity are more important than government policy or incentives.

What brings long-term economic development and prosperity to any area is homegrown businesses. Yet, community leaders are reluctant to invest in startups, and in the hopes and dreams of local dreamers.

Sam Walton faced this situation in Newport, Arkansas, so he left. Fred Smith, the FedEx founder, met it in Little Rock, Arkansas, so he left. Amazon recently initiated a bidding war for its next headquarters. Cities across the nation actively courted this megacompany with no regard for the startups in their communities.

This lack of community support and regard as bonafide businesses requires small farms to go it alone. There are no local supports for small farm leadership, innovation, or creativity. Granted, the USDA may have a few direct market programs, but these programs come with strings attached while moving at government speed. Besides, many local USDA agents don't believe in these programs, which creates an unnecessary success barrier.

Leadership has been, and will always be, a lonely road. That's okay. Leadership is not about fitting in, being accepted, or keeping up with an outdated status quo. Leadership is about turning dreams into reality. Harriet Tubman said it this way, "*Every great dream begins with a dreamer. Always remember, you have within you the strength, the patience, and the passion to reach for the stars to change the world.*"

Farmers are naturally energetic, patient, and passionate people, so it just makes sense that small farmers are dreamers. It is time to move away from the misguided idea that small farms, homesteads, and urban farms are low-skill, tech-free, and economically viable. It is time to embrace that these places require specialized skills, utilize technology, and are financially sustainable.

Be visionary

"The only thing worse than being blind is having sight but no vision." ~**Helen Keller**

Visionaries are dreamers in action. We all dream and have fantasies and desires. There is nothing wrong with dreaming and wanting more. These things keep society moving forward. Susquehanna Trust and Investment Co. knew this when, in 1929, they ran an ad with the headline, *"The dreams of today create tomorrow's realities."* This ad could run today and provides timeless wisdom for small farms.

George Bernard Shaw said, *"Don't wait for the right opportunity: create it."* Creating your own opportunities allows you to build a farm and live according to your own rules, standards, and design. Personal dreams and professional ambitions establish a strong vision of tomorrow's possibilities. The difference between dreaming and envisioning considers current resources, constraints, and reality while operating without boundaries.

Visionaries defy the status quo by writing their own rules. The farming industry clings to antiquated practices, a reason many generational family farms struggle. The USDA reinforces this by providing pamphlets, programs, and educational opportunities to train and educate all farmers in the same way.

The result is an industry in decay and one which shuns innovation while promoting standardization. Many people talk about standardization as if it should be an industry goal. It should not be an industry goal because industry standardization does two things. First, it destroys innovation. Second, it weakens rural economic development and prosperity.

Visionaries dare to be different. In business, differentiation drives innovation and profitability. Small farm differentiation provides positive change and growth. Just as biological systems grow and adapt, economic systems must evolve and adapt. More importantly, industries within economic systems must grow and adjust as well as businesses within those industries.

Leadership is a process

> *"Life is a lively process of becoming."*
> ~**Douglas MacArthur**

A common mistake is treating leadership like a business strategy or a manipulation method when it is a way of thinking, acting, and being. A refrain in many leadership books is the idea of getting people to do things, which is an incomplete view of leadership. A more comprehensive view of leadership requires looking inward and developing oneself before acting outwardly toward others.

The essence of leadership requires looking beyond manipulation strategies. Effective leadership focuses on being our best selves, so we can get the best from others. Sustainable farms (and other businesses) have one thing in common — leaders who lead themselves before leading others.

Leading yourself requires mastering emotions, intellect, and health. It also means that you know what you want to accomplish and, more importantly, why you want to achieve it. As long as people need paychecks, they will comply with directives without putting their hearts into their work. Granted, they will meet a minimal standard, but meeting minimum standards is different than exceeding expectations.

Getting the best from people requires more than a mundane reason for work. A fulfilling mission inspires high-performing people, creating meaning, a sense of accomplishment, and community connection.

People are emotional creatures. Emotions always bring out the best or worst in people. Leaders understand how to harness emotions in a robust practical way. Today, many managers talk about data-driven decisions as if that is the solution to all problems. It is not.

The problem with data-driven decisions is it takes out the most critical variable in business decisions, the human element. Data is essential, but it should not be a substitute for robust decision making. Data is a tool, technique, or guide, but it is not the decision.

Data-driven decisions are nothing more than a reincarnation of Scientific Management, a management approach from the early 1900s promoted by Frederick Taylor. He coined the phrase "time is money" and believed in finding the "one best way" to do a task — items ignoring the human element.

Scientific management, in the beginning, had some successes. Over time this approach led to the workforce's dehumanization and created barriers and boundaries that need not have existed. There were many problems with this management style, including one prevalent and misguided idea that people are naturally lazy.

People are not lazy. If people were naturally lazy, we would still live in the forest, picking nuts off the ground while eating insects. People strive for accomplishment, contribution, and recognition.

When I was a teacher, student decisions were supposed to be guided by the "data." I remember being in more than one meeting talking about a student's performance. Each time I would discuss a student's personality, situation, or interest, I would receive a reprimand because we couldn't see those traits in the data. According to the "experts," I was only to use the data when making student-related decisions.

I never have and never will believe test scores and data determine a person's future or potential. I also do not think that business decisions should be based solely on numbers. Many of the most significant business innovations ignored data, and data drove some of the biggest blunders.

During the 1980s, New Coke became an example of data gone wrong. Coke invested a ton of time, money, and energy conducting blind taste tests to develop a new recipe for its signature product: Coke. The goal was to beat Pepsi's test — a scientifically proven fact that Pepsi was aggressively advertising.

New Coke was released and almost bankrupted an America icon. Had it not been for Warren Buffet's investment and insistence they return to the "old" or "classic" recipe, Coca-Cola would not be around today. The Coke company learned that human emotions are more important than taste.

Decision-making is partly driven by data, partly driven by expertise. Effective leaders rely on more than numbers. Leaders depend on proven processes and practices. Also, they consult with others, think about stakeholders, and are guided by missions, values, and principles when making decisions.

People follow purpose

> *"Work gives you meaning and purpose, and life is empty without it."*
> ~**Stephen Hawking**

Leaders live with purpose. Purpose develops mission, vision, values, and expectations. For a successful small farm, its purpose is everything. George Reed said it this way, *"I don't think you can hit purpose enough as a senior leader… You cannot oversell, overpronounce 'Here's why we're here.'"*

All sustainable farms have a purpose, providing an exciting theme to follow. Besides, purpose creates a meaningful narrative for what would otherwise be mundane tasks. Most importantly, it transforms good intentions into remarkable results.

Having purpose allows small farmers to offer a compelling answer to the question, *"Why do you farm?"* Farming with a goal creates a community by providing people a place to belong and contribute. A place where lofty dreams and idealistic principles come true.

7 Effective farm leader types

> *"Own the leadership style that makes you you!"*
> ~ **Rana el Kaliouby**

There are many different leadership styles and types. While there is no one best way to lead, there are wrong ways to lead. Leadership style is the manifestation of leadership thinking. These styles of leadership are nothing more than patterns of thinking. Here are the seven farm leadership styles.

1. **Idealistic Leaders**. These dreamers want things to be perfect, which in farming is nearly impossible. When farming, things go wrong daily, but that does not require avoiding the pursuit of perfection. Perfection as a goal is excellent as long the person pursuing it realizes it is unattainable.

   Critics chastise idealists because of their big dreams, lofty goals, and grand expectations. Still, it is this group that changes things. Being idealistic is difficult and takes courage, as well as the resilience to bounce back after setbacks.

2. **Persistent Leaders**. These leaders are emotionally resilient and excel at following through. To thrive in a declining, consolidating, and complicated industry such as small farming requires creating and sticking to new realities.

   Persistence allows leaders to move forward in all situations and circumstances. Animals and plants will die, machines will break down, and customers will not follow through as promised. Persistence sustains farmers when these things happen.

Persistence is the physical manifestation of dreams, beliefs, and goals. Being persistent communicates commitment and resolve to yourself and others. Persistence is what gets people through tough times.

3. **Ethical Leaders**. These leaders focus on integrity and have a clear moral compass. Ethical leaders are concerned about right and wrong according to a clearly defined set of corporate values. In the context of small farms, this could be an organic farmer concerned about the use of chemicals, antibiotics, or animal treatment.

   Ethical leaders understand words and actions have the power to create a positive farm culture and build positive working relationships with all stakeholders. They realize this not only makes their farm a better place but also the world a better place.

   People crave fair and ethical treatment at work and in social situations. In a world of declining ethics, being moral makes even more business sense now than ever. Brunello Cucinelli said it this way, "*I believe in capitalism. I need to make a profit, but I would like to do it with ethics, dignity, morals. It's my dream.*"

4. **Fearless Leaders**. Embracing and rushing into change, these farmers are looking for the latest trends, techniques, and technologies to improve their farms. These people seek new ways of thinking, being, and doing and have no connection to the status quo.

   This farm leader is the Richard Branson of farming: a maverick. Mavericks are unorthodox, independent, and unconventional. They realize the most challenging barriers to success are usually self-imposed rules disguised as traditions.

5. **Nurturing Leaders.** They want to grow people as well as things. This leader realizes they cannot do it all, and they need assistance. This leader understands asking and seeking help is not a sign of weakness but a recognition of limitations.

    Nurturing others is about growing people into independent workers. Effective delegation requires employing people who can do a particular task or job without supervision.

6. **Servant Leaders**. They seek to support and serve employees and the community. These leaders engage in self-sacrifice by putting the needs of their community ahead of their own needs.

    Servant leaders are not devoid of self-interest. These leaders seek alignment of personal, corporate, and customer self-interest in a mutually beneficial way, or what the father of modern economics, Adam Smith, called *"enlightened self-interest."*

7. **Visionary Leaders**. They are best described as transformational and strive to create something new, novel, and exciting. Visionaries are similar to idealistic leaders in that they both have lofty goals. The difference is visionaries are not always looking for perfection. These people are more focused on growth and adventure than the industry norm of uniformity.

Visionary leadership is this book's focus. The other styles of leadership are essential and have supporting roles in creating economic viability for small farms. Greatness starts with a vision. Vision will solve problems faced by small farmers, rural America, or urban market gardeners.

People have a primary leadership style or one they are comfortable with. However, not all leadership styles are appropriate for all situations. An essential distinction between good and great leaders is this: good leaders have a primary leadership style they apply to all circumstances. Great leaders know how to match leadership styles to changing and unpredictable conditions.

Nolan Ryan said it this way, "*Enjoying success requires the ability to adapt. Only by being open to change will you have a true opportunity to get the most from your talent.*" Situations and requirements change. When they do adapt, it is paramount to adjust the leadership style to match the current setting.

Grow Enduring Traditions

"Tradition is not the worship of ashes, but the preservation of fire." ~ **Gustav Mahler**

Small farms are usually family homes. Tradition defines families more than any other trait. Families routinely accept new people into the family based on an outsider's acceptance of a family tradition. Families banish relatives because an individual rejects family traditions.

Family traditions use history, rituals, and rites of passage to create a family's identity. Traditions are foundations. They form an emotional center and a sense of place. They become deep roots for massive growth. For a small farm, this allows people to celebrate family greatness while passing the "torch" from one generation to the next.

Traditions guide people to better futures by recognizing the best of their pasts. Traditions define families by creating a sense of belonging and group identity. Extending this concept to a small farm group identity builds healthy organizational cultures and healthy farm communities.

Traditions are malleable. Strong traditions ground people to principles, not practices. New traditions replace antiquated traditions allowing families to grow, adjust, and change as realities change.

Small farms are unique because they are among the few businesses that serve as the family's home and provide the family's income. Practically, there is little distinction between home and business on most family farms. Families form essential building blocks of society. It is more than a cliché to say strong families build healthy communities.

This intertwinement means family and farm traditions are vital to small farm success. This book defines tradition as the passing on of customs, beliefs, and attitudes from one generation to the next. Therefore, small farmers must be intentional when establishing traditions.

Joel Salatin states, "*That a farm is not sustainable until it has financially supported two different generations.*" He emphasizes a common desire to pass the family farm to the next generation. This "passing" does not happen without planning. It is only possible when three conditions exist. First, the farm must be a bonafide business. Second, the current generation must be diligent when preparing the next generation. Third, a member of the next generation must want to continue the farm.

Turning a small farm into a bonafide business demands leadership. It also requires marketing, management, and evolution. Generating revenue requires selling something of value for profit. Therefore, marketing is crucial because small farm profits are marginal. Also, inputs and equipment are expensive. The world is continually changing, and markets are dynamic, requiring small farms to evolve and change with the times, which requires leadership.

Before going any further, it is important to make an overlooked distinction between farm practices and farm traditions. Farm practices are methods of growing and selling products. Farm traditions are ways of life and expressions of purpose and value.

Great farm practices produce revenue-generating farm products; however, farm practices are not farm traditions.

There will be new ways of doing things, whether it is advancement in technology, methods, products, or even marketing opportunities.

Any growing business, including small farms, must evolve and change to meet emerging market demands. This evolution creates sustainable small farms that produce income for multiple generations.

There are two types of small farm traditions: pseudo-traditions and philosophical traditions. Pseudo-traditions are readily observable to casual onlookers, and they are defined by how we farm, what we cultivate, and where we plant. Contrast this to philosophical traditions that require soul searching and digging deep into human motivations. Philosophical traditions describe why people farm, its purpose, or mission, whereas pseudo-traditions describe the superficial.

Small farms that blindly follow pseudo- or superficial traditions may find themselves in bad situations. The practices, processes, and products of 100 years ago are no longer feasible. Even the farm practices, procedures, and products of just 20 years ago are becoming obsolete.

I raise cattle and will use my fellow cattlemen as an example. Many ranchers are reluctant to retail beef directly to individuals, let alone take it a step further by developing prepackaged meals. Instead, many cattle farmers continue to sell animals at auctions or to feedlots while complaining about the obscene money packers and retailers make.

These farmers' complaints identify the solution: direct marketing. It is not just cattle farmers; the same is true about market gardeners who, instead of developing value-added branded products, continue to commoditize them.

This trend limits growth and profitability; however, many farmers conduct business as usual while justifying a lack of progress by labeling it as tradition.

Farmers are mentally stuck and cling to the production economy. A production economy exists for commodity producers. It works quite well for people raising thousands of acres of corn, wheat, or barley. These farmers can leverage economies of scale. It is essential to remember these folks have inherited their vocations, opportunities, and advantages.

A new farmer or homesteader lacks these advantages. It takes capital to reach any sort of economy of scale, which is something most startups lack. To thrive, new farmers must think, act, and market products differently than established farmers.

Successful new farmers adjust their thinking and actions. They shift operations away from production-driven markets and build small farm businesses directed at the experience economy, a much more profitable arena. This market includes people who are willing to pay higher prices and people who seek brands that reflect their values: lifestyle brands. Most importantly, these customers desire relationships with local farmers.

Granted, this is a unique farming approach but one that builds a new road to profitability. Becoming a lifestyle brand requires small farmers to do something they have not done before — build relationships with end-users.

Small and family farms are on the decline, especially those that grow commodities. Leadership can build small farms, even in a declining market, by transforming their business models from commodity producers to experience providers. The key to this growth requires replacing the damaging mantra of, *"We have always done it this way."* to *"We will find a new way, a better way."*

It is a fact that owners of declining small farms spend far too much time talking about the good ole days. These people love to discuss how these latest fads would shock granddaddy or how granddaddy would roll over in his grave if I did _____. The reality is granddaddy would be more upset at losing the family farm because current owners refused to meet the customer demands.

These farmers fail not because of fads, trends, and changing consumer taste; they fail because they follow pseudo-traditions. Pseudo-traditions lack creativity and fail to recognize unique challenges and opportunities. These traditions neglect the underlying emotional needs that drive human behavior. Pseudo-traditions may provide comfort along with an "illusion of security," but this "security" closes minds and limits choices while fostering further decay of family farms.

Pseudo-traditions form the powerful and hypnotic emotional trap called nostalgia. On the one hand, there is nothing wrong with warmly remembering a simpler time or place. On the other hand, holding on to a past or situation that will never resurface is unproductive, unwise, and unhealthy.

This longing is a real-life version of the Mirror of Erised from J.K. Rowling's Harry Potter series. This mirror allows people to see their heart's greatest desire. This magical object would trap people into a fantasy to the point where they neglected the present world.

Nostalgia, like the Mirror of Erised, is bewitching and tantalizing. It does not bring about lasting happiness, results, or reality. Enduring happiness, results, and paradigms come from purposeful action. Helen Keller said it this way, *"True happiness... is not attained through self-gratification, but through fidelity to a worthy purpose."* I cannot think of a more worthy purpose than building a small farm into a sustainable business.

The most effective traditions are philosophical traditions. Philosophical traditions express motivation, define small farms and family purpose, and instill principles. Instead of farming the _way_ great-granddad farmed, focus on _why_ he farmed. Philosophical traditions require explaining, exploring, and examination. These traditions focus on carrying on the underlying motivations, desires, and hopes of our ancestors.

Answering questions such as, "Why did great-granddad farm?" does this. Was it to only feed people, or did he farm to make a better life for his family while contributing to his community? Did great-granddad move to a strange land for a quick fix, or did he search for a long-term opportunity? Did great-granddad build a house just for shelter, or did he create a home?

Humans have moved throughout history to create a better life for themselves, their families, and their communities. I believe my ancestors wanted to provide a better life for their families and to build stronger communities. I believe my ancestors moved for opportunities. Lastly, I believe my ancestors wanted to build homes instead of houses. These are the traditions that are the foundation of my small farm, and these should be the foundational traditions of your small farm.

Philosophical traditions of small farmers

> *"I believe in traditions; I believe in the idea of things being passed between generations and the slow transmission of cultural values through tradition."*
> ~ **Graham Moore**

These inward character traits are ways of thinking, believing, and reasoning. The most profitable and sustainable ones focus on improving self, families, people, and farms. **Small farm leadership is an internal thought process.** Leadership is about doing the right things for the right reasons. Effective farm leaders are good humans who other people respect because of their characters and not because of their titles.

The following five "Es" describe philosophical traditions: enlightenment, education, edification, effort, and engagement. These traditions guided our ancestors as they built our great nation and created the modern world. These traditions are currently missing in many aspects of contemporary American culture, especially in the business culture. Small farms are the perfect place to bring back these traditions.

Tradition of enlightenment

> *"Enlightenment means taking full responsibility for your life."* ~ **William Blake**

Enlightenment started as an intellectual movement during the 17th century. The goal was to develop reason and individualism, two traits many small farmers claim to value but often do not put into action.

Too many small farmers actively fight reason and individualism. They claim to use logic while employing obsolete growing and marketing practices. When questioned about these practices, they tout "tradition" as the reason. They claim to be individualistic by comparing themselves to "city folks" but walk in lockstep with their neighbors without thinking critically about their farm practices.

Effective farm leaders need to develop and rely on critical thinking. Francis Bacon said it this way, "*Critical thinking is a desire to seek, patience to doubt, fondness to meditate, slowness to assert, readiness to consider, carefulness to dispose of and set in order; and hatred for every kind of imposture.* "

Effective leaders seek out and thrive on new knowledge. Knowing facts is good, but it is better to understand how to critique, evaluate, and apply truths. Proper application of facts converts them into prosperity and transforms small farms into successful businesses.

Critical thinking allows leaders to see problems as opportunities. Non-critical thinking happens without intentionality, but critical thinking is intentional, deliberate, and reflective. Critical thinking will enable leaders to view the folly of their neighbors' actions, to see value in new ways of thinking, and to see different paths for themselves.

Critical thinking builds individualism. Individualism has two important meanings. First, it is the principle of being independent and self-reliant. Second, it is favoring individual action over collective action. Filling rural America's leadership void depends on developing independent, autonomous, and nonconforming leaders.

I have never met a farmer who did not claim to be independent or self-reliant, but I also know many farmers whose actions do not back up those words. Too many farmers support the status quo and fail to recognize their farms are businesses. Running a business to fit in with friends and neighbors is bad practice because it stifles innovation and thwarts growth.

Many local farmers scoff at my operation. They mock the look of my weird Japanese cattle, the way I sell my products, my farm's name, and me. These farmers are taking bets on how long I will last and who will buy my land when I leave.

That is fine. These farmers will not pay my bills, support my children, or save for my retirement. I also understand that my success depends on my efforts and not their opinions. Don't get me wrong, I have a few supportive friends in my area. Still, these friends are mostly considered outsiders, just as I am, by people whose families have lived in my area for generations.

My experience is not unique; most farm leaders, especially new farmers, face similar situations. The best response to this situation is to answer the following question, *"What is more important – the success of my farm or fitting in with neighbors?"* I decided my farm's success is more important than fitting in with my neighbors. That is why I do my own thing and grow my own way. The question is, what are you going to do? Are you going to give in to the status quo, or are you going to grow your own way?

Here is a fact: some small farms are thriving. They thrive because an individualistic leader with a vision chooses to farm differently. These leaders purposefully take divergent actions, risks, and paths. They follow Robert Frost's advice of *"taking the road less traveled."* And, as Robert Frost

predicted, they are better off because of it. These farm
leaders intentionally became a different type of farmer, one
following the tradition of enlightenment.

Tradition of education

> "Education is not just about going to school and getting
> a degree. It's about widening your knowledge and
> absorbing the truth about life." ~ **Shakuntala Devi**

Effective small farm leaders are lifelong learners. There
was a time, not long ago, when people learned for the
sheer joy of learning. Granted, some people are active
learners, but unfortunately, that group is declining. Sadly,
too many farmers take pride in their lack of education.

John F. Kennedy said, "*Leadership and learning are
indispensable to each other.*" Learning must be intentional
and focused because small farms face severe economic
challenges and stiff competition from massive multinational conglomerates. As if this was not daunting
enough, there are social and legal pressures from
environmentalists, government bureaucrats, and pesky
neighbors. All of them claim to know better than you and
believe that their desires supersede your livelihood.

I recently read that food manufacturers and processors are
considering replacing American-grown farm products and
farmers. They investigate whether places such as Africa or
third-world countries, where land and labor are cheap and
plentiful, would be more profitable. Whether or not that is
going to happen is up for debate. What is not up for debate
is where loyalties lie.

A small farm leader who deliberately learns will always be
more prepared than a small farm manager hoping for the

status quo when faced with market challenges. Small farm success depends on leaders who are not only serious about education but who are also intentional about learning along with its practical applications.

Education builds the future. Many books and experts talk about the importance of leadership traits. All leadership traits have merits, but one characteristic shared by all effective leaders is a pursuit of learning. Besides improving leadership skills, education is the single most crucial factor for developing a fulfilling, successful, and productive life.

There are two broad categories of education: formal and informal. Formal education comes from schools and provides diplomas, degrees, or certificates that indicate a minimum knowledge level. Informal education is learned from reading books, talking to others, listening to audiobooks or podcasts, etc.

Informal education fills in the gaps. Public or formal education is necessary but incomplete. Professionals such as doctors, lawyers, teachers, realtors, etc., are required to attend workshops, seminars, and other professional development events to supply missing or new facts. Informal education allows people to acquire the knowledge to turn dreams into reality. **Informal learning takes ownership of the most valuable asset a person has: their mind.**

Competitors will copy products, marketing strategies, and processes. The one thing a competitor cannot copy is your mind. Developing one's mind is always a family farm's most sustainable competitive advantage. The mind's content is non-replicable; it cannot be taken away by another. B. B. King said it this way, "*The beautiful thing about learning is that nobody can take it away from you.*"

Education increases vision. Achievement is a function of imagination. Increased education improves vision, which leads to the discovery of choices or options not previously visible. Knowledge allows people to see further, do more, and live better. Jean Piaget said it this way, *"The goal of education is not to increase the amount of knowledge but to create the possibilities for a child to invent and discover, to create men who are capable of doing new things."*

The vision created by education is grounded in hope. Spending time on social media, engaging with neighbors, or listening to talk radio creates an inaccurate worldview. These people make it is easy to assume the world is going to hell in a handbasket, and small farmers are going extinct. There are small farm challenges; however, I disagree that the situation is hopeless. I am inclined to believe the words of George Washington Carver, who said, *"Where there is no vision, there is no hope."*

Complainers and naysayers lack vision. As a group, they lack insight, ideas, and motivation. This is the manifestation of hopelessness, dispiritedness, and professional capitulation. Education cures these ills through building hope, enthusiasm, and engagement. Education replaces complainers and naysayers with advocates and optimists who make the world better.

Vision is a critical trait of entrepreneurship and leadership. Big and bold thinking always has and will create more wealth, jobs, and opportunities than thinking small and scared.

Each decade brings proof of this. At the end of any decade, large businesses exist that were merely an idea only 10 years earlier. Some of these businesses were improvements on existing businesses, while other companies are something entirely new. No matter the case, this new large business began as a person's skillfully executed vision.

Education creates self-awareness. The self-awareness created by education allows people to utilize thoughts deliberately. Independent and directed study enables people to grow their own ways, do their own things, and design their own lives. Understanding people have free will is recognizing intentional choice is personal power.

Viktor Frankl said, "...*the last of the human freedom — to choose one's attitude in any given set of circumstances, to choose one's own way.*" Free will makes this possible.

Deliberate learning increases self-awareness, allowing a person to see more choices, options, and opportunities. On the other hand, a lack of self-awareness inhibits free will while leading people into roles defined by other people.

Leaders reject roles given to them by others by creating roles based on their own desires, dreams, and decisions. Anthony K. Tjan said it best by saying, "*The best thing leaders can do to improve their effectiveness is to become more aware of what motivates them and their decision-making.*" Here are the ten best practices to increase self-awareness.

1. **Have an open mind.** Successful leaders are intellectually adventurous. They actively seek fresh ideas, information, and insights, especially related to mission, objectives, or goals. Also, they are willing to change their minds or courses as new information emerges.

2. **Understand key strengths.** Be confident in what you know. If you excel at a particular task, there is no need to hire someone to replicate your efforts. If

you are bad at a specific job, learn it, or delegate it. Do not ignore it.

3. **Understand key weaknesses**. We all have areas in which we can improve. Leaders are consistently building on and overcoming their shortcomings.

4. **Diagnose key drivers**. Leaders understand internal motivators. Motivations arise from many sources: money, fame, accomplishment, etc. I have my motivators and reasons for work, and you do too.

5. **Develop metacognition**. Metacognition is thinking about thinking. Leaders understand the importance of how to think and what to think about it.

6. **Define boundaries.** As a leader, you are an advisor, supporter, and guide, but not necessarily a friend. Caring about people is important, but caring is not a reason to sacrifice a dream, or in this case, your farm. As a leader, it is vital to define and maintain professional boundaries with people.

7. **Be objective.** Fact-based decisions and interpretations of your and others' abilities become a growth catalyst. A great leader always reflects and self-evaluates. Also, great leaders routinely assess other people's performance and behavior.

8. **Define triggers.** Developing self-awareness allows people to identify situations that drive irrational reactions. Showing and sharing emotions is great, but flying off the handle leads to regret. When stressed out or frustrated, it is better to process feelings internally before sharing with others.

A good practice is to use a journal, diary, or planner to record triggers and responses to those triggers. Recording triggers helps identify the root cause of the trigger, the response, and how to manage it. This process creates personal growth, which improves future decision making.

9. **Create feedback loops.** Feedback loops aim to find errors in reasoning, locate missing information, or discover divergent courses of action. Feedback loops work by creating a situation where people express thoughts while exchanging and developing ideas with others.

   Feedback loops are nothing more than conversations about plans, goals, or actions. This loop is a series of questions and answers designed to guide, refine, and clarify ideas in a manner that creates practical actionable plans.

10. **Understand the process.** Growing self-awareness is a process of questioning motivations, deepening understanding, and increasing perception. Always ask why you are doing a thing, the expected outcome, and what you hope to accomplish.

    This is an application of metacognition. Metacognition and self-awareness are symbiotic processes. Metacognition requires self-awareness, while self-awareness increases metacognition.

Education provides hope. The Pittsburgh Promise, a non-profit organization dedicated to connecting urban children with scholarships, touts *"Education Inspires Hope."* Their objective is to strengthen the region, inspire systemic change, and transform lives. This aspirational tagline works just as well for rural America, small farmers, and urban gardeners as it does for the children of Pittsburgh.

Possibilities inspire hope. Hope is the reason today's succeeding farmers are busy creating new options, inventions, and products. Hope is why farm leaders try new things, take risks, and succeed where other farmers struggle. These actions are a byproduct and creator of hope as well as a self-sustaining cycle.

Education exposes people to new possibilities, which reveals new opportunities. These opportunities allow farms to thrive, even in declining markets. It is a fact that thriving businesses exist in market downturns just as businesses fail in market upswings.

The difference between success or failure is often nothing more than seeing possibilities, having a growth mindset, and holding on to hope. During troubled times, hope allows people to work for a better future. Hope builds energy and inspiration that leads to new products, processes, and practices. Hope is the difference-maker that can save small farms.

Education is action, and action creates hope. Learning is one thing a person can do daily to move closer to a dream. Successful people never stop growing, which is why you should never stop learning. Farmers need education in not only developing products but also in building people, markets, and themselves.

Tradition of evolution

Systems evolve. Today's world is different than it was a century ago. Tomorrow's world will be different from today's. Change used to be slow and predictable, but today change is fast and chaotic. The small farm leadership challenge is anticipating rapid transformation in an industry that produces products slowly.

Evolution is growth, development, and advancement. Without evolution industries, organizations, and people experience death, decay, and deterioration. Many small businesses, as well as family farms, are extinct because they failed to evolve. It is easy to blame competitors such as Amazon, Walmart, Tyson, etc., for small business and rural America's decline, but that blame is misguided.

The blame lies with small businesses and family farmers who do not recognize fresh players as serious competitors. Any business or farm established before a new competitor had three advantages: customers, resources, and reputation — three things taken for granted by complacent managers.

Charles Darwin said, *"It is not the strongest of the species that survives, not the most intelligent that survives. It is the one that is the most adaptable to change."* This quote explains the difference between established businesses failing and startup businesses succeeding. Amazon is a prime example of succeeding by applying modern technology to old catalogs. Many well-known retailers, such as Sears and Toys "R" Us, ignored technological advances and changing customer preferences.

Darwin's quote exemplifies many farmers' problems: the misapplication and direction of challenging work, tradition, and uniformity. The reality is taxing work does not always pay off; sometimes, it only creates an illusion of progress.

Granted, nothing gets done without it either. Gordon B. Hinckley said, *"Without hard work, nothing grows but weeds."* This will always be spot-on. Still, for arduous work to be sufficient, it needs direction, purpose, and growth.

Right traditions are priceless. For a farm to be sustainable, traditions must be purposefully selected and intentionally created. Too many struggling farmers use self-limiting and outdated traditions. These traditions require replacement with new barrier-breaking growth-creating traditions.

Many agricultural traditions encourage uniformity. Successful small farmers must break away from uniformity. All farmers, but especially small farmers, must evolve from commodity production to farm brand production. There are five levels of farm evolution. They are ranked here from the lowest to the highest level.

- **Level 1: Commodity**. These products are things such as plain beef, pork, grain, produce, etc. At this level, there is no difference among products. Producers of commodities are subject to taking only what the market offers. At this level, farmers produce more of the same product, which creates downward pressure on prices.

- **Level 2: Product Differentiation**. The next level is product differentiation. At this level, farms develop reputations for quality or specific products. Customers recognize a farm's name, but customers lack an emotional attachment to the farm itself.

Customers are willing to pay a little more but not much more to buy from this farmer.

- **Level 3: Service Differentiation**. This step is the foundation of brand loyalty. For a small farmer, service differentiation includes elements such as product delivery and customer service. Small farmers can use service as a method to attract more customers. This level creates even greater control over product pricing.

- **Level 4: Customer Expectations**. Meeting and exceeding customer expectations creates deeper customer relationships. At this level, farmers grow products or provide services for customers other farmers are unwilling or unable to deliver. Going organic or all-natural are examples of this level. Customer loyalty increases, and farmers have even greater price control.

- **Step 5: Farm Community**. At this level, customers become part of the small farm's community. Customers genuinely buy into the farm's mission and vision. Here customers become advocates for the farm, and farmers have much control over price.

Evolution believes looking forward builds a better tomorrow than dwelling on the past. Rajeev Suri says it this way, "*Don't hold on to the past; it won't help in moving forward. Dare to dream big.*" Far too many farmers lament about the good ole days while claiming farming's best days are long gone, a sad but true statement for those who believe it.

These farmers are stuck on Level 1 farming: commodity production. **Economic prosperity today and in the future**

requires small farmers to evolve beyond producing commodities. Small farm leaders must develop a farm community that delivers on customers' needs and wants.

Other farmers believe that the best days are yet to come. A true statement, again, for those who believe it. Thinking the best days are coming supplies the optimism necessary to keep farming, keep working, and keep dreaming.

An optimistic mindset creates and nurtures ideas; it is the birthplace of innovation. William Pollard said it this way, *"Learning and innovation go hand in hand. The arrogance of success is to think that what you did yesterday will be sufficient for tomorrow."*

Today's farm leaders must be innovative. Innovation is not jumping on board with every new fad, piece of technology, or trend. It does mean looking at the overall economy and analyzing consumer wants while making difficult complex decisions. Change may be difficult, but failing is excruciatingly painful, if not lethal, to your business.

Tradition of effort

"Continuous effort — not strength or intelligence — is the key to unlocking our potential. "
~ Winston Churchill

Without sustained effort, nothing happens. We all know people who claim they are going to start working on their goals tomorrow. These people claim they are waiting for the time to be right or to be inspired. We also know the people who make those claims never get anything done.

Our ancestors valued effort, which, by definition, is a vigorous determined attempt. Their determination built farms, industry, and communities. It is a principle, stating meaningful accomplishments only come from sustained and directed effort.

Farms are the best place to raise kids because farms have endless opportunities to teach children the principle of effort: tireless work and commitment. Farms allow children to pursue entrepreneurial activities and learn the fundamentals of business first-hand and in real-time.

The modern, easy, and instant gratification world has diminished the importance of effort. Working long and hard for accomplishment has been replaced by immediate results and easy money. This ease of gratification isn't healthy, and as we will see shortly, it may be deadly.

The lack of effort required for survival, combined with the modern world's ease, has created a complacency trap. Today's world makes it easy to be comfortable, and who doesn't like that? I know I do, but I also understand comfort brings danger. It is not only a danger to me but also to my children; it is a danger to you and your children.

As parents, we need to fight this. As parents, we need to be teaching children the importance of work. We do this by example; as a parent or farm leader, you set the tone for the level of effort you expect from your children or employees by the quantity and quality of your own work.

Wild hog trapping illustrates the complacency trap. Catching a wild hog requires baiting a trap. The problem is the wild hogs' sharpened sense of awareness, and any slight divergence to routines or environment alarms them.

Trapping wild hogs requires making them complacent. To train wild boars to be complacent, you must change their behavior and environment gradually. The first step is making it easy for the animal to eat. According to the "Wild Pig Info" website page from the Mississippi State University-Extension, this is called pre-baiting.

Hogs love eating effortless meals. The pre-baiting process takes two weeks or longer, depending on the hog's experience. Previously or nearly trapped pigs are cautious and are reluctant to join the hogs who are enjoying a leisurely meal.

Eventually, the seasoned hogs will cede to jealously. The easy meal the other hogs are enjoying is too much of a temptation to the "wise" pig. It leads them to disregard prior knowledge or experience by following the others into the baited area. These hogs willingly overlook what they know, and, as a result, they make a fateful decision.

The slow process of trap building begins when pigs are comfortable enjoying their free meal. Nondescript, uninteresting, and big traps work the best. Trap building is slow and methodical, starting with one panel. As the pigs become accustomed to this first section, the trapper adds panels until there is only one way in and out of a large sturdy pen.

Finally, the trapper adds a trap door set open for easy access. Skilled trappers are patient and wait for the group (sounder) of hogs to eagerly enter the enclosure. A hasty entry indicates pigs are ready for capture. The trap door is triggered, allowing for the sounder trapping.

This metaphor offers valuable life lessons. The most important is farmers must avoid complacency traps. A typical complacency trap for farmers is growing contracts.

There are other traps, but this particular trap requires attention. A growing contract appears attractive. It promises an income and simplifies marketing; however, when inspected, it is a one-sided agreement that transfers all the risk to the farmer while moving all the profits to the processor.

Growing contracts are excellent for large corporations but bad for small farmers. Growing arrangements, especially poultry, are notoriously bad for growers. Poultry contracts require farmers to purchase all inputs and sell all their outputs to the same corporation, which sets the buying and selling prices.

Years ago, farmers rushed into these contracts like wild hogs chasing a free meal. In the beginning, producers enjoyed the relationship, but over time minor contract modifications, by design, created agreements that benefited the corporation at the farmer's expense. This subtle change to the deal was slow and gradual, just like constructing a wild hog trap.

This first change may have been a new or different piece of equipment, a unique blend of feed, or a new lighting system. One of these things at a time may have had little or no impact on the farmer's bottom line. Over time, these minor changes created significant problems for poultry farmers.

It is as if these corporations learned from wild hog trappers. These corporations lured in farmers with big promises, dreams, and incomes. This trap often snared even the most experienced and educated farmers. In short, these corporations manipulated the market and took advantage of the farmer's emotional attachment to their farm and land. While this system created value for corporations and their stockholders, it lowered life quality for rural America and family farms.

For corporations, it is about creating and using systematic power for economic gain. When farmers are free to buy inputs from the open market and to sell to the open market, farmers win, and corporations lose. On the other hand, when corporations control the process from beginning to end, they will always win, and farmers will lose.

The corporations have monopolized the food system. It was done through slow, steady, and sustained effort, which "baited" farmers. Granted, farmers willingly and eagerly took the bait, which is why farmers have shared responsibility in today's situation. The food economy's current state is a sad situation, with many farmers stuck with legally enforceable yet destructive contracts.

There are rare exceptions, and a few large farms may benefit from this arrangement. Generally speaking, small farmers with growing contracts are suffering. Many of these farmers spent generations scaling up their operations to a point where they are dependent on these contracts for survival. Publicly traded companies "baited" farmers.

I do not know any small farmer who is happy with their growing contract. Each farmer claims to feel trapped, and nearly all of them claim they are not making the promised money. They all regret it, but at the same time, they do not know what else to do. Sadly, the farm is on the line for many; they have lost their sense of independence while experiencing a heartbreaking situation.

These contracts have eroded marketing resourcefulness. These farmers are painstakingly hard-working and honest to a fault. Corporations, concerned about stock prices and not a farmer's livelihood, trapped these farmers into serfdoms. Instead of earning a decent income and preserving family land for the next generation as promised, they got something entirely different.

There is a solution for farmers who are responsive to the needs and wants of customers. In other words, there is a solution for farmers who are willing to vertically integrate: a process of product development and selling direct — the same approach used by large companies.

As farmer leaders, it is crucial to put in the effort necessary to be successful. The future of small farms depends on the individual efforts of individual farmers. Small farms will be saved by farmers who avoid the traps set by large food companies. It will be a hard-fought David and Goliath story, but saving family farms and rebuilding rural communities is worth the effort.

Tradition of engagement

> *"We all have dreams. But in order to make dreams come into reality, it takes an awful lot of determination, dedication, self-discipline, and effort."*~ **Jesse Owens**

The definition of "engage" provides the best introduction to this tradition. The word engage originates from the old French word "gage," which had two important meanings. First, it meant to pledge oneself to do something. Secondly, it is active involvement in something.

Farm leaders need to "pledge" or dedicate themselves to farming. Farming is a lifestyle occupation and is best-suited for people who cannot separate work and play, not because they are workaholics, but because of their joy for farming.

Before the industrial revolution and the development of scientific management, ordinary people found meaning in work. In the early 1890s, scientific management developed an emphasis on efficiency. It led to more productive systems, which replaced the need to hire skilled ardent people with those who could do a single mundane task.

The specialization of labor and assembly line work created a workplace shift. Crafts or tradespeople whose labor commanded a premium salary were replaced by unskilled people, or people willing to do a simple repetitive task for next to nothing.

For much of human history, a person's vocation was indistinguishable from the individual. Take the development of last names as evidence of this fact. Originally, last names described people's occupations or talents. For example, a blacksmith named John became John the smith or John Smith.

Being engaged in work means life by design. People, including you, were not destined to spend their lives in a cubicle or office somewhere. That concept applies equally to entry- or line-level positions, whether it is a factory, restaurant, retail store, or a host of other meaningless jobs.

Owning and running a small farm is one of the few occupations that allows people to be something of their own design, purpose, and passion. It reconnects people to a time where a person's work was indistinguishable from the person while building an exciting and rewarding future.

Aligning a person's occupation with emotional and spiritual needs is the cornerstone of resilient leadership. The only way for anyone to self-actualize is to be fully engaged, engrossed, and enraptured in one's daily work. Leaders who are faithful to themselves become creative psychologically robust self-actualizers, which are required to build sustainable small farms.

The push for efficiency, standardization, and increased profit has created an unnatural work-life balance. Today, people must compartmentalize work, family, play, and pleasure. Life is short. It should not be all work and no play, and for sure, life must include family.

I advocate for a vocation where it is difficult to distinguish between work and play because work is enjoyable and meaningful. Small farms are places where work, recreation, and leisure intersect.

Being an effective farm leader requires engagement in all aspects of the farm business. Most farmers find it easy to focus on farm chores, tasks, and similar concerns but find it difficult to concentrate on marketing, managing, and leading.

Farm marketing is as essential as any other farm activity. Farm leaders must oversee their marketing efforts because good marketing is the difference between selling a commodity and selling valuable branded farm products.

Many small farmers have a misguided notion of the role of marketing. The misconception is that marketing is about manipulation; it's not. Marketing is about sharing your passion for your farm with the world. It connects a farm with people who are looking for farm products.

Generally speaking, effective small farm management is sporadic. Let me explain. On the one hand, most farmers do a fantastic job of managing planting, growing, raising animals, and operations. On the other hand, many farmers struggle with managing and leading people.

Effective small farm leadership creates dependable capable people. People make farms operate efficiently, making life easier for farm owners. Accomplishing this takes time, commitment, and forgiveness. Farmhands make mistakes. When this happens, the most common advice is to fire them and hire someone else, which is terrible advice.

The current farmhand should have been the best person who applied for the job. If you did not select the best person for the job, that decision is on you. You made the hiring mistake, not the farmhand. Typically, the best course of action is to train, grow, and mentor the individual. Some situations require immediate dismissal; however, generally speaking, it is better to develop people instead of dismissing them.

Training and development of people takes leadership. Managers may be able to get short-term results that fail to create long-term sustainability. Leaders, on the other hand, build the future. Training and development are the most effective pathway to creating a sustainable future.

Managing traditions

Traditions are a critical aspect of small farm culture. Small farm culture is deceptively complex. On the surface, it looks simple, and easy to create and explain. However, developing a robust small farm or organizational culture is complex. It grows more complex as each new person (customer or employee) joins the operation.

Culture and traditions guide workplace behavior, ethics, and dedication. All too often, farmers and small business owners will dismiss this as nothing more than soft, fluffy, and touchy-feely nonsense that has no place on a farm. That approach is wrong.

Small farms, particularly family farms, must invest in culture. Small farm leaders need to intentionally craft culture by identifying and communicating values, mission, and purpose to all members of that farm's community. Other farms can and will imitate your products, processes, and practices, but the one thing that is not replicable is culture.

As a farm leader, it is imperative to assess farm traditions. Whether you realize it or not, you follow certain traditions or rituals. Some of the traditions are helpful, and some are hurtful. As a leader, the goal is to identify beneficial traditions and build on them while replacing harmful traditions with new valuable traditions.

Not all traditions are useful; not all traditions are bad, but all traditions need analysis. One essential leadership function is to define and refine farm traditions to support the farm's purpose.

The traditions kept or modified must support the farm's purpose and fulfill its vision. Just because daddy or granddaddy did something or conducted business in a certain way should not be a constraint or obstacle for growing your farm, your way.

We all have worked somewhere and had to perform a task in a certain way that did not make sense. When we questioned it all too often, we were told, *"We have always done it this way."* This answer always has and always will be the absolute worst answer.

In the history of work, not a single person capable of abstract thought bought into that answer. I know hearing that lame answer always annoyed me, and I bet it has always annoyed you, too. Therefore, why would anyone ever use that response?

When anyone asks you about a practice, policy, or process and you give that annoying answer, it is time to reflect. If you cannot provide a concise rationale for clinging to a particular tradition, you must question it.

Leaders start traditions. Growth, personally or professionally, requires ending meaningless practices while creating new beginnings. Effective leaders are continually growing, learning, and exploring. Ineffective leaders stick with the status quo and go down with the ship without trying to save the ship.

New traditions bring new opportunities to small farms. New traditions keep the ship (your farm) afloat while moving in any direction of your choosing. New traditions are new beginnings that build on your previous experiences, expertise, and education.

As you develop new traditions, people will resist. People fear the unknown, uncertainty, and unpredictability. As a farm leader, it is vital to prepare people for change. To help people transition and adjust to new traditions, follow these nine steps.

1. **Assess**. Survey your farm, local economy, and national trends for opportunities. Compare your findings to your farm operations, and plan accordingly. Also, listening to employees and customers provides a different viewpoint of your farm. Their insights may offer clues as to current or potential problems, issues, or opportunities.

2. **Plan**. Develop a plan of action that will take your farm from its current situation to its desired position. Proper planning is essential. It establishes direction, sets priorities, and guides actions. It is more than a cliché to say that failing to plan is planning to fail.

3. **Explain the need for the new tradition.** Explain the business need. Always remember small farms are small businesses, and businesses must adjust and adapt to stay relevant.

4. **Explain the rationale for the new tradition.** People need to buy into the decision making and be guided through the "why." They don't necessarily have to agree with it. Many will not, but communicating the rationale for the "why" is the first and most crucial step for creating lasting change.

5. **Acknowledge the challenges in developing, defining, and delivering the new tradition.** There will always be a learning curve, new ways of thinking, and the development of new habits. This step takes time, energy, and focus. Recognizing and preparing for challenges is a better option than hoping things will "work themselves out."

6. **Develop reward systems, both formal and informal.** People respond to incentives. Developing change initiatives requires developing and aligning new incentives. The key is to reward the new behaviors and attitudes you are looking for while disciplining the ancient practices, beliefs, and views you are eliminating.

7. **Monitor employee behavior, and provide immediate feedback when expectations are met or violated.** Positive praise when people meet the new expectation communicates the importance of the new tradition.

8. **Provide ongoing training and emotional support.** People are emotional. We all are, and to deny human emotions in a business setting is a recipe for disaster. People develop emotional bonds to things, processes, and events.

9. **Follow through with the new tradition. Plans are easy to make but difficult to execute.** The number one reason organizational change in any setting fails is that management fails to follow through.

Starting traditions is a long-drawn-out process. People will test leadership and organizational commitment to any new practice, even ones they suggested. Small farm leaders must make the new tradition a part of everyday work life.

This task requires commitment and pursuit as if the farm's future depended on it because in many cases, it does.

As mentioned previously, some traditions must go or at least be changed. There are traditions, patterns of thinking, and practices that need to die. Even the best families, farms, and businesses do harmful, dysfunctional, and useless things.

There is no need to cling to a non-resurrectable past, or expressly, a past that is holding back profitability and growth, and endangering a farm's future. Letting antiquated traditions fade into history is more about looking forward and future building. The past is gone. The present has replaced it, which is yielding to the future. In short, effective leaders work toward building a better future instead of resurrecting an obsolete past. There are four types of farm traditions.

1. **The strong destructive tradition**. It is like a thistle, deeply rooted, difficult to manage, and dangerous. These outdated traditions bankrupt small farms that dig into maintaining the status quo. Immediately eliminate these practices.

2. **The emerging harmful tradition**. These traditions are like weeds in that they emerge slowly and gradually erode effectiveness. All organizations, including farms, cut corners, make mistakes, and poor decisions. When left unchecked, these minor hiccups can become destructive unhealthy habits.

3. **The emerging productive tradition**. These traditions are like annual garden plants. They express innovative ideas, products, and services. These traditions require nurturing and attention

and provide immense potential for the farm's future.

4. **The strong productive tradition**. These traditions are like an established orchard that produces an abundant yearly harvest. They create a sense of community, belonging, and purpose. These traditions sustain a farm through good times and bad.

Emerging Productive traditions

Expresses new ideals

Provides a road map for new direction

Needs deeper embedding in the farm's culture

Are challenged

Strong Productive traditions

Create sense of belonging

Productive

Clearly understood

Expresses clearly defined values

The future

Strong Destructive Traditions

Rooted in the past

Serve no purpose

Limits thinking, vision, and action

Destroys the farm from the inside out

Emerging Destructive Traditions

Bad habits

The result of entropy

Focuses on external conditions

The Past

Grow Self-Investment

"Knowing yourself is the beginning of all wisdom."
~ **Aristotle**

This section uses the term self-investment instead of self-improvement. It better represents the building of your most valuable asset: you. Learning and growing is an investment that pays a lifetime of dividends, or as Ben Franklin said, *"An investment in knowledge always pays the best interest."*

There are no naturally born leaders; they develop through intentional action. Looking at today's birth announcements proves this point. A hospital's birth announcements are nothing more than a list of names, not a list of occupations, titles, or roles. People grow and develop into leaders by investing in the following traits: competence, efficacy, authenticity, appreciation, hope, motivation, commitment, and discipline.

Investing in competence

"Leadership shows judgment, wisdom, personal appeal and proven competence."
~ **Walt Disney**

Competence is more than a simple skill; it is a deep understanding of a given task's nuances. Competence requires the necessary knowledge to do a job and a sense of why a mission is essential, the role it plays, and how to troubleshoot problems when they arise. There are five levels of competence.

1. **Skill development.** Skill development is the lowest level of competence. Learning to ride a bike offers a perfect example to explain skill development. When first learning to ride a bike, the learner starts with training wheels and coaching, providing real-time feedback. This pattern continues until the learner can ride without training wheels.

2. **Understanding.** Building on the bike-riding example, the learner understands how a bike works and the basic principles, along with a few facts. At this stage, the learner graduates from a simple one-gear bike to a 10-speed bike, mountain bike, or other specialized bike.

3. **Proficiency.** At this level, the learner knows enough to teach other people how to ride. Teaching others is imperative for the learner as it embeds the process at a deeper level.

4. **Evaluation.** Learners are better able to evaluate bikes to determine what works best for a given situation. Reaching this level of competence improves decision-making skills.

5. **Creation.** This is the highest level of competence. This level converts learners into creators. The most advanced learners can build bikes, make improvements, or create new applications. For example, a person with this level of competence may convert a bicycle into a generator to watch TV or run some other appliance.

Competence is essential for leadership but so is expertise, capability, and gumption. Being a competent leader does not mean you know how to do everything. No individual is an expert on all issues. That is okay. What is essential is a sound understanding of your core business: farming.

Farm leaders must understand farm practices, processes, and principles. Also, farm leaders must understand the difference between leading and managing. The small farm community has many great managers but only a few great leaders. This leadership void is an opportunity for individuals desiring to lead, who want to accomplish great things and rejuvenate a struggling industry.

Investing in self-efficacy

"In order to succeed, people need a sense of self-efficacy, to struggle together with resilience to meet the inevitable obstacles and inequities of life."
~ **Albert Bandura**

Efficacy is fact-based positive thinking. Self-efficacy allows people to look at complex tasks and chores as challenges to master. In contrast, people lacking self-efficacy look at the same work as a reason to surrender individual hopes and dreams.

Self-efficacy is a byproduct of accomplishment as well as a critical ingredient of achievement. The more successes experienced by a person, the more it builds self-efficacy. Mastering a task, skill, or practice always develops a spirited sense of efficacy. This process is contagious as an accomplishment in one area of life is evidence of competence, capability, and capacity. There are nine efficacy traits of farm leaders.

1. **Moral compass.** Effective leaders have self-chosen and internalized values rather than externally imposed values. Internal values are self-selected,

which allows leaders to avoid unrealistic demands or expectations of others.

A clear compass is a shield against peer pressure by creating what is known as the achieved identity: an authentic individual. This identity allows leaders to scrutinize and build personal attitudes, beliefs, and standards without limitation, nor fear of what others may think, say, or do.

2.   **Self-evaluation**. Self-efficacy requires objectively taking inventory of one's strengths and weaknesses. Self-assessment facilitates farm leadership as it allows leaders to better define the purpose, scope, and direction of the farm. Families intertwine with small farms like no other business. This evaluation enables leaders to better integrate professional, financial, and family goals into this amalgamation.

3.   **Proper social modeling**. For leaders, seeing similar people succeed is motivating. This modeling works because witnessing people prosper, who started on equal or lesser footing, proves the American dream is alive and well for those willing to take action.

I have always loved rags-to-riches stories, whether fictional or real. These stories provide optimistic and practical social modeling. Social modeling is learning by watching others. Unintentional social modeling leads to disastrous results; whereas, intentional social modeling leads to successful outcomes.

4.   **Maverick**. Create new pathways while ignoring industry norms. All industries struggle between people who want to maintain some outdated status

quo and people who wish to disrupt industry norms. History supplies proof that success always favors those willing to take a new or different course of action to get extraordinary results.

5. **Independent**. Leaders have the fortitude to resist peer pressure from neighbors, friends, and family. People who claim to be independent but walk lockstep with their neighbors while making fun of and criticizing others who think or act differently are the norm in the small farm community.

   Independent farm leaders do not need to criticize different people. These leaders seek to understand and learn from people with divergent points of view. Leaders realize success in any industry can come from the most unlikely places, which is why they are searching for solutions in the most unlikely places.

6. **Determined**. Leaders approach problems as a personal challenge to overcome. They don't quit working until their dreams become a reality. The demanding work that is farming requires sustained effort. Not being able to sustain this effort is the number one reason people fail in small-scale agriculture.

7. **Inquisitive**. Dive deeper into farm activities, processes, and practices. Efficacy requires learning, which is nothing more than questioning. People with efficacy ask questions, even "stupid" questions.

8. **Intentional meanings**. Our responses, emotions, and interpretations of situations either increase or decrease our self-efficacy. Intentionally labeling is

more productive than unintentional interpretations. If nothing else, deliberately assigning meaning to a problem creates some control.

Johnny Cash said, "*You build on failure. You use it as a stepping stone. Close the door on the past... You don't let it have any of your energy, or any of your time, or any of your space.*" He is right; words are powerful and create our version of reality.

9. **Creativity.** Strong leaders are creative. One thing all small farmers have in common is limited resources. Creativity distributes resources diligently and industriously while ensuring economic application to the farm's mission.

   Developing creativity improves problem-solving skills, which are vital on a small farm. Creative farmers look at things differently and see opportunities others overlook. Innovative farmers are better able to see connections hidden from uncreative and struggling farmers.

Efficacy begins in early childhood; the feedback kids receive from parents, peers, teachers, or others molds their sense of efficacy. This formative development is empowering and creates people who view the world with wonder, accomplishment, and excitement. These people believe in possibilities.

If this is reminiscent of your upbringing, congratulations, you have an essential advantage. However, if this is not the case, hope exists. Many people had a childhood like mine — one with family members mocking one's abilities, criticizing efforts, and ridiculing dreams. There is good news. Self-efficacy is developable at any age.

I have many examples of things I wanted to accomplish, experience, or explore, only to hear people like "us" don't do those things. The earliest big dream I had was to be an Egyptologist. In the fourth grade, I read a graphic novel on Egyptian history: I was intrigued. I shared this with my grandparents, who said that was about the dumbest thing they have ever heard, and I needed to "grow up."

A few years later, I learned about pesticide enzyme inhibitors in agriculture science class in the eighth grade. I was intrigued and thought this would be a great job, and I could be a great farm scientist. I reasoned if I could learn to identify the proper enzyme for various crops, chiefly produce, I could make a lot of money and help a lot of farmers. I shared this with my dad, who said, "*Smart people become scientists, not people like you.*"

These two examples are not isolated; they were the norm. Sadly, this exists in the homes of far too many rural and impoverished people. This cycle holds both individuals and communities imprisoned by a misguided belief, believing success, accomplishment, or the "good life" is for others.

This widespread belief has created a self-imposed caste system in much of rural America. Too many people believe that to move up the social-economic ladder requires cheating, taking shortcuts, and manipulating others. People temporarily get ahead with those methods, but that success is fleeting, limited, and unstainable at best.

Rural America needs to replace its self-imposed caste system with an advancement system, a growth system, or an opportunity system. Rural America must return to the pursuit of life, liberty, and happiness by striving to actualize the American Dream. This is carried out on the individual level by dreamers with efficacy.

When individuals develop self-efficacy, they not only change their lives for the better, but also they alter the trajectory of their families and communities. It is a deliberate choice that requires breaking down the most challenging obstacle a person can face: the barriers of disbelief.

Breaking down these mental barriers is the first step in developing self-efficacy. I know. I left my family and its dysfunctional traditions behind. When I did this, not realizing it at the time, I developed self-efficacy and became a leader. I confess I did not know what I was doing, where I was going, or the effort it would take to sever family ties. When I think of my immaturity, paradigms, and beliefs, I cringe at how bad they were; however, I have no regrets about leaving the situation.

That "cringe" or problem awareness is difficult to manage. It is painful to admit something is wrong. It is more painful when it deals with our thinking, beliefs, or habits. Accepting something is wrong and that things will improve is the genesis of personal growth.

I was ignorant when I first went out on my own. All I knew was there were two basic types of people, the "us" and the "them." The "us" crowd took the "easy classes" in high school, and we were not supposed to use our brains. Our destiny was to stay behind, work on the farms, and pursue blue-collar jobs while settling for middle-class wages. Struggle for survival was our destiny.

The "them" crowd took challenging classes and were headed to college, which led to professional lives. This group used their brains, not their brawn. Their destiny was to move away and fall off the edge of the world. At least, we thought that because when they left Pine Snag, they never returned. Their destiny held good jobs, fancy cars, houses, and a comfortable life.

In my senior year in high school, I started hanging out with the "them" crowd. I decided to go to college my senior year not because I wanted to go but because my new friends were going. I also went to college because I knew I had had enough of the "us" crowd, and I wanted to join the "them" crowd.

My family was not supportive. For the next several years, they kept asking when I was going to stop doing that "college" thing and join the "real world" and get "real experience." Not only did I finish college, but I also earned two graduate degrees and a graduate certificate.

Here is an excellent place to point out that college is not for everyone. More importantly, college is not the only pathway to success. Education is quintessential, and college provides it; however, higher education doesn't hold a monopoly on learning. For me, it developed my sense of efficacy, independence, and resilience. Three very critical qualities my family did not instill in me.

Investing in character

A small farm is a business, and as with any business, the most valuable asset is its brand. A business leader's character is the foundation of a brand. Leaders create expectations with their actions. When a leader acts with integrity, so will employees. When a leader works with deceit, so will employees.

For long-term success, there is no substitute for character. As Jon Huntsman, Sr. says, *"There are no moral shortcuts in the game of business or life. There are, basically, three kinds of people, the unsuccessful, the temporarily successful, and those who become and remain successful. The difference is character."*

Character is the only way to build sustainable relationships, whether professional or personal. All farm leaders have the following FARM character traits.

- **Follow through**. The only time you should follow is when you follow through. It is nothing more than keeping commitments. Eddie Rickenbacker offers the following advice, *"I can give you a six-word formula for success: think things through — then follow through."*

- **Accountability**. Farm leaders accept responsibility for mistakes. Leaders must never transfer blame to followers under any circumstance. Nothing disempowers an employee quicker than throwing them under the bus. Nothing empowers an employee more than assuming responsibility for their mistake.

- **Realism**. Farm leaders need to deal with facts, truths, and evidence and not speculation, conspiracy theories, or fantasy. A small farm is a real business in the real world. Farm business decisions must use truth, facts, and evidence as guides.

  The small farm or homestead industry is full of fringe personalities who peddle conspiracy theories, fantasy, and fallacies. These people are entertainers who are making money based on fear and sensationalizing obscure events. It is why making decisions based on their talking points **always** leads to failure.

- **Morality**. Moral leaders are concerned with right and wrong. They have principles and unyielding values they communicate to their followers. These internalized behaviors guide decisions, determine actions, and build organizational culture.

Building a multi-generational sustainable farm requires building generational character. The founding or current leaders must have the unquestionable character to instill strength and integrity into the following generations. Remember, morality, ethics, and integrity build a farm's reputation more securely than good marketing.

Most small businesses, including small farms, do not survive longer than the second or third generation. I believe it is because the generations after the founding generation lack depth and breadth of character.

These people may be honest, but character is more than honesty. **It is a multi-dimensional concept that includes commitment, excellence, consistency, and appreciation.** Farm leaders who want heirs to be successful with the farm must instill these traits into the next generation. Failure to do this is treating the following generation like bowling pins by setting them up to be knocked down.

Sound character is a sustainable competitive advantage. The world is fluid, dynamic, and chaotic. Success in any business is challenging. Every day companies start, grow, decline, or fail. It is a brutal world. No one cares more about the success of your farm than you.

Thriving in this environment requires small farms to be competitive, but not in the sense most people think. Too many farmers think of competition as a head-to-head or a win/lose game. It is more profitable to regard competition as excellence, creativity, and significance.

I am about to make two statements that many authors and consultants will disagree with. I may even get a few bad reviews for expressing them, but I stand by them. First, many authors and consultants are misguided and incomplete when talking about competitive advantage.

Experts typically speak of competitive advantage as competing on price, service, or developing a niche. While these actions are essential, they are also superficial, obvious, and copyable, so as a result, they lack sustainability. Building these items around a farm's mission, vision, and values while building customer relationships makes them sustainable.

Customer relationships require the three T's.

- **Trust**. Trust is certainty in another person's behavior. Trust seasons over time. It is the result of several interactions in various situations. Trust is a byproduct of knowing people do not seek to take unfair advantage of each other.

- **Time**. There is no substitute for time. Time allows people to see past the superficial first impression and look deeply into a person's soul or spirit. Time reveals flaws while highlighting virtues. It takes time for relationships to strengthen.

- **Testing**. Testing people is natural in all relationships. If you are a mission-driven farm, people are going to test sincerity. Sadly, today's world is full of charlatans looking for a quick dollar, which is why customers will check your authenticity. The key is not to take it personally. Like you, they have been disappointed many times before.

Second, focusing on head-to-head rivalry repels opportunities faster than it attracts new customers. Competition is real, pervasive, and intensive. This harsh reality is not a license to *steal* customers or to sabotage a neighbor or other small farmers — many of whom are just trying to earn a living, such as yourself.

It is entirely acceptable to *win* customers from whoever is not providing the same quality products and services that you are. The goal is to gain customers by offering customers more value for their limited dollars. It is why competition has a net benefit on society. Winning in business is more about developing a better business practice, process, or product than it is about sabotaging another person's livelihood.

Approaching business as a head-to-head competition is operating with a scarcity mindset, a misguided belief that views life as a win/lose situation. A person with a scarcity mindset sees the world as a place of limited opportunities, resources, and growth.

This person believes getting their fair share means depriving others. These people view themselves as victims, and as a result, make decisions out of fear, anger, and resentment. The most dangerous and limiting trait associated with the scarcity mindset is the misguided belief people have little or limited control over their outcomes. These people externalize their locus of power by believing their situation controls their decisions.

As a result, people with a scarcity mindset will slander neighbors while also engaging in malicious acts against neighbors. These people's tools are manipulation, lying, and bad-mouthing. Tools used for a few extra dollars today. Sadly, these people will sell their souls for a short-term temporary gain while excusing their bad behavior as "just business" or "this is the way it is."

Excuses do not justify bad behavior. If anything, it highlights the intentionality of their actions and the lack of quality character. The only benefit to others is that this behavior shows a person's real character: a person whose soul is for sale.

Contrast this to a person with an abundance mindset. This person believes the world offers plenty to all. This optimistic outlook views the world as full of resources, possibilities, and opportunities. This person builds their future, believes they have control over their environment, and takes ownership of actions.

A resourceful person views small farmers as collaborators, customers as business partners, and employees as farm members. This person makes decisions based on hope, facts, and courage.

Small farm success requires resourcefulness.
Resourcefulness is developable — an internal quality. As a group, they are crafty, persistent, and adaptable. They handle new situations skillfully with purpose. They are the backbone of any industry and our country.

Both the scarcity (victim) and abundance mindsets reflect character. These inward qualities become foundational for your small farm business. Building on the foundation of victimization is akin to building a house on the sand. It will only stand until the first storm. Whereas building a house on resourcefulness is similar to building a house on solid rock. It will withstand even the most powerful winds.

Investing in appreciation

> *"Gratitude is a currency that we can mint for ourselves, and spend without fear of bankruptcy."*
> ~ **Fred De Witt Van Amburgh**

Wisdom can come from anyone, anywhere, and at any time. The guiding thought for this section came from my son's piano teacher. He explained to Calvin the importance of having the right mental attitude when practicing the piano and all areas of life.

The teacher recounted a story of how, as a kid, he thought he was powerless. Like many people, he thought he was a byproduct of his circumstance and environment. He shared how he had spent the bulk of his early life stuck in negative thinking.

This negative thinking was limiting, and while he didn't realize it at the time, he just wasn't a happy person. One day it all changed when he was the tallest person to be cut from his basketball team. He experienced the normal emotions: anger, jealousy, resentfulness, bitterness, etc. Emotions that feed negativity, drain energy, and destroy motivation.

His parents, hoping to cheer him up, took him to the zoo that weekend. At the zoo, he saw a kid his age in a wheelchair enjoying the zoo and having a great time. He said his first thought was, "Why is that kid happy?" Then he thought it must suck being in a wheelchair. He said his next idea was it felt good to be walking, and his day instantly got better.

He said a "light bulb" went off in his head as this was the first time he paid attention to his thoughts. He realized he could change his feelings and emotions by changing his thoughts. He put it this way, *"I decided to put my mind in charge of my mood."*

The small farm leadership lesson is to always be appreciative and thankful for whatever life brings. This intentional thinking is made possible by metacognition, which is thinking about thinking.

Being appreciative of circumstances, even the so-called bad ones, creates control of thoughts and feelings. It may not change the current situation, but it is a start to something better. Viktor E. Frankl, an Austrian neurologist, psychiatrist, and Holocaust survivor, said, *"Everything can be taken from a man but one thing: the last of the human freedom — to choose one's attitude in any given set of circumstances, to choose one's own way."*

Viktor Frankl said how many people (rightfully so) gave up and accepted their doomed fate in concentration camps. He also shared how certain heroic prisoners would offer hope to other prisoners. The difference, Viktor claimed, was a difference in thinking because there was no difference in circumstances.

Thinking is the difference between freedom and liberty. True freedom comes from within; it is a mindset. This mindset prevents defeat even in the face of death. This mindset recognizes confinement and loss as real constraints. It also harnesses the power of the human mind to improve any situation by merely thinking differently.

Thankfully, the conditions discussed in Frankl's book aren't the norm in modern America. It will stay this way if enough people respect the rights of others. Leaders must be vocal advocates of the right to pursue life, liberty, and happiness. It is the best defense against this manner of intolerance, violence, and evil.

The most desperate conditions in rural America exist in the minds of rural Americans. Rural Americans need to free themselves from the chains of despair, hopelessness, and ignorance. Rural America needs small farm leaders who have freedom of the mind: people who embrace the human endowments of optimism, hope, and spirit.

Small farms are the best places to live, but something will go wrong daily. The goal is to be in control of your attitude when things go awry. Attitude and mood are both a choice. I know it is a choice. I have chosen to have bad attitudes, something we all do, and I have also chosen to have good attitudes, something we all do.

Changing attitudes will fix the issue internally. This internal fix has external benefits. Primarily it allows the mind to switch its focus from what is wrong to how to fix it. There are eight steps to cultivating appreciation.

1. **Language**. According to linguists, the words, grammar, and metaphors people use shape perception. Farm leaders need to use language that builds an appreciation for current situations intentionally.

2. **Journal**. Keep a running gratitude list. Some days, it is easy to forget your blessings, but as the Sunday school song says, "*Count your blessings, name them one by one.*"

3. **Purpose**. A leader's purpose is everything. Understand farming motivations and drives. It makes farming fun, enjoyable, and rewarding. History is driven by our ancestors searching for the meaning of life.

4. **Reminders**. Keep a list of accomplished goals, objectives, or milestones. There will be setbacks, obstacles, and other hardships. Reflecting on accomplishments is a tangible and tactile reminder progress is happening.

5. **Share**. Share your fortune with others. It helps other people because you become an example of what is possible, and this interaction builds a supportive network. It comes with a warning. Share with people who are positive thinkers, motivated, and opportunity-minded.

6. **Assist**. Help others who are less fortunate. Kindness and helpfulness is always the right thing

to do. Helping less fortunate people makes it easier to see how blessed you are.

7. **Faith**. Believe things are getting better. Believing in a higher power helps with this but so does self-belief. The knowledge that you can change your situation is empowering. Faith is really about expecting things will get better. The rationale or reason for that expectation is not nearly as important as having that expectation.

8. **Celebrate**. It is not a crime to treat yourself. Celebrations are an act of appreciation and thankfulness. Moreover, it is fun, rewarding, and motivating. Celebrations, more than anything else, communicate organizational and cultural values.

Investing in motivation

"I think it all comes down to motivation. If you really want to do something, you will work hard for it."
~ Edmund Hillary

People follow purpose and passion, not position. Being self-motivated is the absolute best way to motivate others. When you are enthusiastic about your farm, work, and mission, people will support your efforts. Creating a compelling purpose for your farm and backing it with passion attracts loyal customers and dedicated employees.

Motivation lays the groundwork for turning dreams and aspirations into reality. Experts discuss goal setting and achievement as if they invented the concept. The pervasiveness of goal-setting literature has turned SMART Goals, goal-setting, and goal-getting into meaningless clichés. The jargon used around goals has reduced goals to nothing more than wishful thinking.

Goals lack action, so they seldom generate results. Principles such as mission, vision, and purpose drive effort, which is why they drive achievement. The ambition provided through motivation is more powerful than writing a goal down on paper.

Instead of focusing on goals, it is better to develop processes, systems, and benchmarks. It works better than goal setting because processes guarantee daily action. A sound system includes tools for reflecting, reassessing, and redirecting as needed. Lastly, benchmarks measure the distance traveled while keeping you on track.

Motivation is the mental energy that makes things happen. Motivated leaders create new products, practices, and processes. These leaders revolutionize industries, create new realities, and build sustainable enterprises. This energy allows leaders to handle setbacks, overcome obstacles, and maintain direction.

Leadership motivation must be intrinsic. The difference between external and intrinsic motivation has to do with its staying power. External motivation is short-lived, while internal motivation has its owner's life span.

Daniel Pink said, "… *intrinsic motivation — the drive to do something because it is interesting, challenging, and absorbing — is essential for high levels of creativity.*" These qualities are vital for small farm leaders and indispensable for building a sustainable business. The high level of creativity discussed here is critical to small farmers because it allows for optimum resource investments.

Small farm creativity comes from intrinsic motivation.
Intrinsically motivated people are dreamers and thinkers.
Creativity is a practical application of optimism, hope, and
intelligence.

Intrinsic motivation is developable, and there are eight
ways to build it.

1. **Alignment**. Intrinsic motivation is an internal
   process, a way of thinking that works only when
   objectives, behaviors, and values are aligned. As a
   leader, it is vital to intentionally select values that
   support goals and objectives.

2. **Emotional intelligence.** In other words, control
   your emotions. Intrinsic motivation brings with it
   positive emotions. When beliefs, values, and
   behaviors are aligned, life feels right. The reason is
   endorphins are released, creating a healthy
   productive addiction.

3. **Time out.** Take time to rest, reflect, and rejuvenate.
   Farming lacks the structure many other jobs offer,
   and many times the farm is the home. Throw in the
   fact that there are always farm chores, and it is easy
   to be overwhelmed; however, take time out to
   enjoy the farm, family, and life.

   Schedule downtime into the workday. Remember,
   farm chores are always going to be there. Friends
   and family will not always be there. Don't neglect
   to feed the animals or ignore emergencies, but
   labeling the cans on a shelf can wait for a rainy day.

4. **Be active.** Develop interests outside of farming. It
   could include the property; for example, hunting
   and fishing are hobbies you can pursue without

leaving home (assuming you, like me, never want to leave). It could also include being active in the community, such as attending church, volunteering, or anything that keeps life exciting and meaningful.

5. **Share**. Sharing with other people builds relationships. It is crucial to have a supportive network that shares the same personal and professional passions. Sharing, especially success stories, is emotionally, spiritually, and physically healthy.

   Farming is often stressful, and sharing emotions and feelings keeps people emotionally healthy. Depression is a killer. According to the Centers for Disease Control and Prevention, farmers are 1.5 times more likely to commit suicide than their urban counterparts. The best prevention for suicide is proper mental health, and this begins when farmers share their emotions and feelings.

6. **Celebrate**. Research shows that celebrations boost emotional health. All farms are a work in progress, and reaching milestones is a cause for celebration. These celebrations do not need to be elaborate if they are meaningful. Jack Welch says that many businesses don't celebrate often enough. He is right.

7. **Mastery**. Doing a good job is its own reward. There are endless farm and farm-related tasks, which means there is always something to learn. I learned HVAC because I want to install and repair my coolers, central heating, and air. Next, I am going to learn welding or diesel mechanic basics.

There is always a new skill set to acquire that can benefit your farm. This fresh skill can reduce expenses or become an additional revenue source. Still, the real benefit of learning things is the emotional wellbeing that arises from the process.

8. **Feed it.** I ate lunch today, but later today, I will be hungry. Just as we feed our bodies, we need to feed motivation. Leaders feed their inspiration, which can be as easy as reading an internet meme or as complicated as taking a college-level class. Whatever you choose, it must be regular and stimulating.

Investing in commitment

"Commitment, belief and positive attitude are all important if you're going to be a success..." ~ **Donald Johanson**

Small farm leadership commitment is loyalty to a mission or purpose. It is a decision to stick with a project, idea, relationship, or course of action after the evaporation of novelty and excitement. Quitting is easy. Anyone can do it at any time. The temptation to give up on a dream is powerful. It provides temporary relief and maintains the current status quo. On the other hand, the struggle to achieve something substantial, significant, and lasting is painful.

People seek pain avoidance. It is a normal response; however, giving up provides temporary relief. Over time, that false sense of satisfaction becomes painful regret, which can last a lifetime. Long-term thinking allows leaders to avoid a lifetime of pain because they know it will be worth it in the end.

Commitment forms vigorous habits, which govern outcomes, determine destiny, and create patterns. Habits determine everything. It is not what we do occasionally that determines our results. It is what we do daily. I grew overweight because I ate fast food frequently without adequate exercise. I didn't lose weight by occasionally skipping a meal or working out. I lost weight by changing my habits.

Habits create our realities. As William James says, "*All our life, so far as it has definite form, is but a mass of habits...*" Habits have a powerful influence. Good habits always bring good results, while bad habits bring bad results. For example, an exercise habit paired with the pattern of proper eating keeps a person healthy. On the other hand, a habit of couch sitting, excessive beer drinking, and eating fried food makes a person unhealthy.

All people have the power to change their futures by changing their habits. We all have habits. Some habits are implicit (unconscious), and some are explicit (self-chosen). Effective leaders develop effective habits, which are nothing more than routines, processes, and actions directed at specific objectives. There are seven steps of habit development.

1. **Assessment**. Assess your current habits. Make a list of what is working and what needs to be changed. When assessing habits, focus on triggers and responses. This first step is concerned with habit identification and awareness.

2. **Evaluation**. It is the extent to which a habit is working. It is different than assessment because evaluation is about determining whether a practice or routine is beneficial. Also, this is about understanding pattern motivation or habit drivers.

3. **Decision**. Nothing happens without a decision to act — leadership decisions center on organizing, planning, and executing plans.

4. **Action**. Start small, simple, and selective. Focus on no more than two or three habits at a time. It is plan execution, and as with all farm activities, nothing will go as planned. Taking on only a few changes at a time will allow people to monitor and adjust as needed.

5. **Reflection**. Ask what is working and what isn't. Make adjustments as necessary. When things go wrong, there is no need to beat yourself up. Turning a setback into learning creates progress.

6. **Reward**. Habits must have a benefit. Reward yourself when making progress. Taking time to enjoy improvement helps you to feel good about yourself.

7. **Consistency**. Twenty-one days is all it takes for a habit to be developed or changed. The goal is for a new behavior or pattern of thinking to be automatic. Once you stop thinking about doing a thing, you can focus your mental energy on other issues.

Developing habits comes from learning, thinking, and doing. Habits determine success or failure; therefore, deliberately develop habits.

Investing in self-discipline

> *"It was character that got us out of bed, commitment that moved us into action, and discipline that enabled us to follow through."* ~ **Zig Ziglar**

Cultivating discipline is a self-discovery and improvement process. Everyone claims to have rules they live by, but many people fall short of their so-called rules. Leaders are different. Leaders have carefully developed practices, non-negotiable standards as a decision and behavior guide.

The leadership expectation is control over things. It is impossible to control people, processes, and practices if you cannot control yourself. Self-mastery or discipline is foundational. It is control over thoughts, emotions, and attitudes.

Things go wrong daily on small farms. Anyone who has farmed for more than a day knows this. I plan for things to go wrong, and I am seldom disappointed. When self-mastery and discipline are present, I can define what happens in productive ways. There are seven steps to building self-discipline.

1. **Intentionality**. To be intentional in the context of self-discipline is to oversee one's decisions, focus, and direction.

2. **Alignment**. Leaders square values and behaviors. We all have stated values we don't follow. Your actions expose your values and reveal discrepancies; therefore, it is crucial to make deliberate actions and values align.

3. **Reflection**. We all mess up, and reflecting on our shortcomings helps us identify why and where we fell short and what we can do differently in the future.

4. **Removal**. Avoid distractions, temptations, and triggers — including people.

5. **Forgiveness**. When you mess up, don't regret it. Too many people are misguided about the idea of living without regret. They view living without regret as living without consequence, which is a mistake that can lead to long-lasting remorse.

   Self-forgiveness is an integral part of self-kindness and care. Flaws are part of who we are, as well as talents, strengths, and skills. Self-forgiveness allows people to define themselves by their positive attributes and not their shortcomings. Mistakes and bad decisions happen. Neither are permeant setbacks. Just learn from them and move forward.

6. **Emotional fortitude**. Leaders must resist temptations. It is easy to give in to peer pressure, which is the opposite of leadership. Emotional fortitude is courage in the face of adversity, sticking to an unpopular decision. It is faith that allows leaders to stick with decisions and do what is right at the right time without hesitation.

7. **Prearrangement**. Leaders know how to respond before they are in a situation. One of the beautiful things about the human mind is the ability to visualize events before they happen.

Grow a Farm Visionary Mindset

Without vision, small farms disappear. There seems to an unlimited supply of news articles and reports announcing the death of small farms. This decline has been happening for decades, making one wonder why a rational person would join or invest in a declining industry?

Visionaries embrace challenges and are enthusiastic risk-takers. **They are adventurers who will save small family farms.** Small farms are perishing not because of competition but because farmers are opportunity-blind.

On average, granted, small farms are declining, but that doesn't mean your small farm dream has to die. There are thriving businesses in any declining industry; just as in booming industries, there are struggling businesses. It is not the economy or industry that determines individual success as much as it is the vision of individual leaders.

Others don't do it this way

"Peer pressure and social norms are powerful influences on behavior, and they are classic excuses."
~Andrew Lansley

Visionaries challenge conventional wisdom and industry norms. Retail icon Sam Walton said it this way, *"Swim upstream. Go the other way. Ignore the conventional wisdom. If* *everybody else is doing it one way, there's a good chance you can find your niche by going in exactly the opposite direction."*

Following industry conventions limits possibilities, reinforces preconceived notions, and clouds judgment. For example, Aristotle, who died in 322 BC, developed a gravity theory that stated more massive objects fall faster than lighter objects. This "obvious" concept was conventional wisdom for more than a thousand years until Galileo put it to the test.

Galileo challenged conventional wisdom. He wasn't content with accepting the status quo, which is why he conducted his Leaning Tower of Pisa experiment. This experiment proved objects accelerate at the same speed when falling, disproving Aristotle's theory of gravity.

Just as Aristotle's misguided theory limited scientific discoveries and advancements for more than a millennium, current conventional wisdom creates problems and limits small farm growth. Today's farmers must follow Galileo's example of challenging the ways things are done instead of following the tradition of the Aristotle supporters who strive to maintain an erroneous status quo.

Conventional wisdom has created an industry that favors processors, wholesalers, and prominent players. It is a system that turns a farmer's work into a commodity. Today, most agricultural markets are oligopolies, if not monopolies, making it difficult for small players to compete according to industry expectations, norms, and practices.

Besides, conventional wisdom has to lead to overspecialization. Today, many farmers produce just one or a few products for only one or a few customers. It creates a divide between farmers and their products' end-users, a division offering no farmer benefits.

The fact is farmers, especially industrial farmers, are one of the few businesses offering a minimal number of products to a handful of buyers. Most companies succeed because they offer multiple products or services that add value to their multitude of customers — the opposite approach of industrial farmers.

Small scale farmers can and should offer multiple products and services. It requires the development of farm-branded products instead of growing commodities. This approach is quite different from the "grow big or get out" paradigm used by the factory or industrial-scale farmers and promoted by the USDA.

The government makes it difficult for farmers to brand products. For example, the USDA uses conventional wisdom to create and maintain commodity-based markets instead of value-added markets. Also, state health departments limit access to locally grown food by claiming farmers processing their products will kill customers. Still, small farmers must face these challenges if they are going to thrive.

Ignoring conventional wisdom creates opportunities.
People ignoring conventional wisdom include dairy farmers who are crafting artisan cheeses. Other examples include protein farmers who direct-market meat, horse farmers who offer trail rides, and produce farmers who create value-added products. Many of these farmers are new farmers who face ridicule and criticism from established farmers who are more than happy to tell these people they are farming wrong.

These new farmers are proof one doesn't need to come from a family of farmers to be successful. The only requirement to succeed is a dream to follow, a desire to make it happen, and relentless devotion to its manifestation. These farmers secure the future because they are creating the future. Following conventional wisdom brings three problems.

- **First**, conventional wisdom maintains the status quo. Following the status quo only benefits industry leaders and large multinational corporations. These mammoth players do not care about you or your farm. As a matter of fact, all the big players in the agricultural community are actively pushing small farmers out through vertical integration.

- **Second**, conventional wisdom is restricting. It is nothing more than a set of limiting norms, rules, and expectations. It is important to know industry norms as this gives insight into building a niche currently ignored by the industry.

  Remember, it is your small farm and your dream! So, you are free to make your own rules, decisions, and goals. Pablo Picasso summed this up perfectly when he said, *"Learn the rules like a pro, so you can break them like an artist."*

- **Third**, conventional wisdom is obsolete. The world continually changes, making adaptation necessary. Sadly, many farmers have not adapted to changes in the marketplace. This lack of adjustment has allowed mega-corporations to write rules that favor them.

Growing your own way requires independence. As you try new and different things, neighbors will tell you, "That's not how it is done, at least not around here." As a farm leader, you need to decide if you want their results or different results. Do you want to adjust to their expectations, settle for their limited attainments, or live your dreams?

Farm vision development

> "Vision without action is merely a dream. Action without vision just passes the time. Vision with action can change the world." ~ **Joel A. Barker**

Vision is an expression of values, beliefs, and desires. A tenacious misconception is being visionary is about industry transformation. It is not. It is more about personal progress, evolution, and a commitment to developing and expressing an authentic self.

For small farm leaders, there is no distinction between personal and professional accomplishment. Therefore, farm vision begins with what an individual farmer wants to accomplish. The most beautiful thing about owning land is it is a canvas for farmers to unleash their creativity. Granted, there may be codes and regulations to follow; however, for the most part, owning land creates freedom.

We all have dreams, hopes, and aspirations, some of which are even delusional; however, dreams are not visions. Dreaming is great. Dreaming is healthy, which is why people dream as they sleep.

Dreams lack understanding and constraint awareness; they are free from real-world constraints and consequences, something everyone has. The two most common limitations are time and money, but other obstacles could include deficits in knowledge, skill, and technology.

Farm visions are realistic versions of dreams. Vision develops small farm potential grounded in current resources, constraints, and opportunities. Farm vision is alertness in action, deliberate planning, and purposeful work that takes advantage of current market opportunities.

A small farm's vision is the starting point for branding, which is a vital business activity. Large companies such as McDonald's, Coke, Pepsi, etc., focus on branding because it works. It works because it creates an emotional connection with customers. Farm leaders can make a personal connection with customers. Something large corporations struggle with is creating that personal connection, and this is why farm leaders must focus on branding and building community.

I do not believe that large corporations necessarily care about their customers. Corporations may care for them as a group but not as individuals. More importantly, this care comes from utility rather than genuine concern. Seriously, are you convinced any large company cares about you or me?

People desire human connections, concern, and caring. The internet and social media were supposed to help bring people together. They didn't. Instead, technology drove people into smaller tribes that may feel larger on the surface, but in reality, they isolate more than they connect. Small farms offer the perfect solution to this problem. Small farms can become places of refuge, connection, and caring — places to experience community.

It begins by sharing the farm vision with customers. Customers are inquisitive. They want to know who you are and what you stand for. **A farm's vision is a beacon for people who share its values, beliefs, and passions.** Inviting these people into the farm creates loyal customers. They will invest in your farm by buying more profitable farm-branded products instead of buying cheap commodities from big box stores.

Mission development

> *"Every person above the ordinary has a certain mission that they are called to fulfill."*
> ~ **Johann Wolfgang von Goethe**

The mission is an actionable version of the vision. When a small farm is mission-driven, it has a sincere devotion to a task, goal, or outcome. A farm's mission is evident; it is actively pursuing a noble pursuit with enthusiasm, intensity, and devotion.

Many organizations overthink and over-complicate when creating mission statements. I have been involved in far too many committee meetings creating and drafting mission statements. Typically, these meetings created a wordy document that people did not understand, remember, nor practice.

Having a mission is required. It is essential, but because something is important doesn't mean it must be complicated. As you create the farm's mission statement, resist the temptation to complicate the process. Simply define the mission in a few sentences or phrases based on values, beliefs, and vision.

It is your farm! Make your mission statement **your** mission statement. Unless you are taking money from someone else, there is no need to involve others in the process. I know that many experts talk about consensus-building to gain buy-in from others. It has been my experience that, that seldom happens. In fact, it has the opposite result. When I have been involved in the process, there has never been a 100% harmonious agreement. It has never even been close. I agree that 100% of the time, there will be disgruntled, annoyed, and generally frustrated people.

Develop your mission, then select people based on their ability and willingness to commit to the mission. It is much easier to choose people who agree with and are excited about the mission than to convince people the purpose is paramount.

Johann Wolfgang von Goethe said this about having a mission, "*Every person above the ordinary has a certain mission that they are called to fulfill.*" As you create your mission statement, remember farming is a noble pursuit that leads to an extraordinary life.

Mission statements must be sharable; therefore, they must be written. It is a great marketing and people-management tool to include the mission statement everywhere possible.

As you write your mission, keep the following tips in mind:

- **Short and simple**. The best mission statements are concise and say no more than needed.

- **Compelling**. Mission statements are inspirational to you and the people you select to join you on the farm's journey.

- **Timeless**. A farm's mission statement needs to be future-focused.

- **Principled**. Principles are fundamental truths, beliefs, and ideas that withstand the test of time. A mission statement based on a current fad will provide only short-term results, at best. Lasting and sustainable mission statements are principle-based.

- **Adaptable**. Markets and customer preferences will change. As small farms grow, they change. As you, your farm, and market opportunities develop, be prepared to adapt to the current demands and resources.

Think big, start small

> *"For me, the winning strategy in any start-up business is, 'Think big but start small.'"* ~ **Carmen Busquets**

It is easy to criticize and demonize large businesses. However, that doesn't change the truth at one point: these businesses were just someone's dream that started small. It also does not change the fact that I want my small business to grow large.

I want my farm to grow and prosper; you should want the same for your small farm. There is nothing wrong with growth, success, and popularity. There is no reason or rule stating prosperity requires sacrificing core beliefs, values, and mission.

Thinking big does not mean worldwide domination; however, it should be big enough to create a sustainable business that supplies a substantial income. Money is essential for many reasons; the most crucial reason is it presents choices.

Thinking big and starting small is really about taking inventory of your current assets, resources, and environment and using that inventory to create economic prosperity. The best defense against large corporations, competitors, and customer changes is growth.

Growth allows for adaptions to market conditions and niche development. Small farms need a niche. There will always be people who do not like large multinational corporations; these people are any farm's core customers. Look for opportunities to connect with these people while developing a niche around their wants and needs.

It seems that I am saying to ignore a large part of your potential market; I am. Growth companies in any industry focus on their clearly defined and targeted core customers. Applying this concept to small farms creates a clear path to both increased sustainability and profitability.

Small farms have limited resources, and developing a niche creates the focus necessary to get the best results for your efforts. This approach allows the development of a foothold or leadership position in the local market. From here, farms can leverage resources into growing into a sustainable business.

Starting small allows you to start where you are. Opportunities abound, and small farms must identify them. In any area, there are financially secure people as well as economically insecure people. The financially stable create value, whereas the financially vulnerable make excuses. A fundamental difference between these two groups is leadership.

Leaders take stock of their assets and situation to figure out what value-added innovations can be devised to take on the industry giants. Followers settle for what is in front of them with no concern for improvement or no desire for anything better.

Innovation

> *"When the winds of change blow, some people build walls and others build windmills. "~* **Chinese proverb**

Innovation creates wealth. This is the best economic engine for small farms and rural economies. Milan Kundera puts it this way, *"Business has only two functions – marketing and innovation."* The same thing can be said for any farm that desires growth and sustainability.

Innovation requires thinking beyond basic farm practices. Farm operations are essential, but growing products, whether plant or protein, is just the first step.

There are seven best practices of small farm innovation.

- **Look around**. Start by analyzing and examining other industries. Food-based businesses are the clear starting points. Researching restaurant and food trends is a glimpse into the next big thing. This provides insights into new ways of delivering, supplying, and marketing farm products.

- **Listen and observe customers**. What are customers telling you that they like and want? Also, as you visit grocery stores or restaurants pay attention to people interacting with products like your farm's products. What are these people searching for? And, how can you provide it for a profit?

- **Watch competitors.** This could be other small farms or large corporations. The small farms you are watching should not be limited to your area but across the world.

- **Learn new things.** Innovation is the juxtaposing of knowledge and creativity. Do not limit your learning to just farm practices, but learn about marketing, technology, or anything else that can create value for your farm.

- **Continuous improvement.** Always be thinking of ways to improve processes, practices, and products. There are two ways to create value for customers: reduce expenses or add value to existing products and services.

- **Baby steps.** There is a misguided idea that innovation must be big, flashy, and disruptive. The fact is it doesn't. Minor improvements are progress. We all love giant leaps forward and instant gratification. Still, those massive leaps are not daily occurrences, nor should they be.

- **Problem solve.** Business success is more about solving problems and supplying solutions than creating the next big idea. Focus on what people need or want, even if they do not know they need it.

Intentional focus

Focus determines results. We all know that thinking and believing you are going to be sick can make you sick. This thinking doesn't invite viruses, bacteria, or toxins into the body. It does, however, weaken the immune system so that an average amount of toxins become harmful.

On the other hand, thinking you are getting well is necessary for the healing process. Once again, there is a physical reason for this. Good thoughts release hormones and chemicals that increase white blood cells, which combat toxins.

The same is true for many things. I knew a guy once who believed he was going to divorce the girl he was marrying. He even bought a book on how to prepare for a divorce before he got married. He got a divorce.

Focus is a force that creates the physical manifestation of human thought. Concentration is more than a gateway to thinking; it is a gateway to results. It is the foundation of all habits. As previously discussed, habits control behaviors, which in turn determine results.

Focus awakens the subconscious. Intentional focus directs the subconscious to learn new tasks or to work on complex problems. This fact explains why we had to consciously think about applying the gas and brake pedals when we first learned how to drive. And how, after a few years, we can accelerate and brake without conscious effort.

Leaders understand this, and therefore they intentionally focus on what they want to achieve. As a former math teacher, I can tell you that the difference between students who excel in math and the students who don't is usually a matter of focus and belief.

The same could be said for the difference between small farm owners who excel and those who do not. Agriculture is full of people who focus on what is wrong with the industry, so they fail. These people say things and believe things like people don't care about where their food comes from, or they can't compete with the big guys.

Agriculture needs leaders who focus on opportunities, believe small farms are legitimate businesses, and that enough people do care about where their food comes from. This requires the following three steps.

- **Clear your mind**. This takes practice. Clearing your mind is more than not thinking. It is about letting go of problems, anxieties, and distractions while focusing on solutions, the good, and the positive. Many people find meditation, deep breathing, or hypnotic music helpful.

- **Have a place**. This could be the kitchen table, in your vehicle, on the tractor, walking through your field, etc. It could be multiple places, but there must be spaces associated with deep thinking.

- **Unplug**. We live in an overconnected world. Phones and other electronic devices keep people distracted and pull attention away from achievements, fundamentals, and plans.

Fail forward

Learning from your mistakes is failing forward. Mistakes happen. You are going to forget to shut a gate, plant too early or late, or put off weeding for a few days too long, along with thousands of other things big and small. Failing forward ensures these mistakes or accidents are not wasted. Denis Waitley describes it this way, *"Failure should be our teacher, not our undertaker. Failure is delay, not defeat. It is a temporary detour, not a dead end."*

Being comfortable with failure is one of the most important things a leader can do. As a teacher, the most challenging concept I taught was that mistakes are nothing more than effort evidence. Students who learned this lesson found mathematics easy; those who didn't struggled.

Eloise Ristad stated, *"When we give ourselves permission to fail, we, at the same time, give ourselves permission to excel."* Increasing our comfort level with mistakes and failures allows us to discuss those mistakes with others, reflect on them, and develop new approaches for the next time.

There are five strategies that turn mistakes into learning.

- **Assess.** How did it happen? Was this deviation from some standard or norm? What principle or value was ignored? And why?

- **Reflect.** Why did things go wrong?

- **Reframe.** It's not a mistake but a lesson learned.

- **Make a list.** Decide what you will do differently in the future.

- **Grow.** Farm life is about growth. Many farmers understand their job is to grow things while forgetting to develop themselves or others.

Failure is a temporary event, not a permanent situation. When things don't go as planned, learn from it and move on. Failures are in the past; whereas, success is in the future. Small farm growth and progress is never linear. It is a jagged and even backward process at times, but those who stick with it succeed.

Growing People, Growing Farms

*"From my very first day as an entrepreneur, I've felt the only mission worth pursuing in business is to make people's lives better." ~ **Richard Branson***

Abraham Maslow said, "*A musician must make music, an artist must paint, a poet must write, if he is to be ultimately at peace with himself. What a man can be, he must be.*" Leaders intently applying this truth create pathways for workers. The goal is to encourage people to become who they were meant to be, even if that path leads an employee to a new career with a different organization or industry.

This idea that people must grow into what they need to become is not just some crazy hippy-dippy psychobabble nonsense. It is a free-market economic principle. In robust free-market economies, people are not only allowed but encouraged to pursue self-interest or individual dreams.

This is a modern application of Adam's Smith "invisible hand," which is the unseen, unmanaged, and chaotic force that shapes economies. According to <u>The Theory of Moral Sentiments</u>, written in 1759, when individuals seek their own self-interests, they create unintended but positive social benefits.

When individual freedoms are stifled, everyone suffers. This affects small farms at the business level. It is safe to say that when a business limits personal growth, it hurts, restricts, and weakens itself and society. Therefore, leaders must help people become what they want to be, even if that something is outside the farm or industry. Not every employee will be a lifer; not only is that fine, but also it is preferable.

Leaders grow people. This investment in growth is the most sustainable pathway to building a business. People are indispensable for a farm's success. Competent people make farming easier. Growing people ensures standards are met, customers are satisfied, and owners get an occasional day off.

The right person in the correct position is freedom. A persistent misconnection states if you want something done right, do it yourself. That is just plain wrong, as well as limiting. Jesse Ferrell, a mentor, always said, "*The key to getting rich is having something or someone making you money while you sleep.*"

Small farms experience financial independence when employees work independently. This independence just doesn't happen. It happens when people work with purpose, pride, and passion. When a leader inspires people to work hard, diligently, and independently it creates a situation where leaders can make money without being physically present.

It should not be confused with a laissez-faire approach to farming. Leaders are aware of the big picture and all the moving parts. Followers lack this awareness and, as a result, require guidance, direction, and instruction. The goal is to employ people who can work both independently and interdependently to reduce friction while increasing efficiency among these moving parts.

For example, a small farm leader can only attend one market, auction, or other sales event at a time. Having multiple people working in numerous locations simultaneously increases revenue and profitability.

Selling products at multiple sites on the same day increases overall revenue. There are added expenses when selling at various locations; however, profits are created if income is greater than costs.

The key to increasing sales and creating farm growth is dependable staff. This starts with the hiring process. Hiring is a crucial business decision, and is the most essential human resources decision. It is also one practice that many farms neglect.

Hiring right

> *"The employer generally gets the employees he deserves."*
> ~ J. Paul Getty

Hire for organizational fit, and train for skill. A person who believes in a farm's beliefs, values, and mission is always a better choice than a technically proficient person. Training for expertise or technical know-how is more effective and efficient than changing a person's beliefs and attitudes.

This contrasts with the traditional small farm hiring practices. Too many farms, and other businesses, place excessive emphasis on skills while unfairly defining candidates in terms of experience, education, or expressed skill set.

People are much more than what is listed on a résumé or job application. Besides, people can do much more than they have done in the past. People drive business and ought to be treated as resources. Yes, people need paychecks, but all things equal, people embrace workplaces that values, nurtures, and inspires.

Hiring begins with a small farm's mission, values, and beliefs. Leaders select people based on organizational needs and purpose; whereas, managers hire based on job descriptions and technical skills. Hiring solely on position and technical skill communicates to the new hire that they have limited responsibility and accountability. Hiring for purpose demonstrates to the new hire that they have meaning. It tells the person they have an obligation beyond a narrowly defined role.

Effective leadership views the hiring process more as a philosophy than as a set of rules or practices. When I worked in human resources, I followed industry practices. That was a mistake. The goal was to protect the organization from lawsuits. A better plan would have been to select people with growth potential and cultural contribution.

Most organizations assign growth to the sales and marketing team. I disagree with that approach. I believe business growth is the responsibility of all units. Growing businesses thrive and, as a result, are better able to weather the crisis and economic downturns much better than stagnate or declining companies. Hiring for growth and potential is a better philosophy than following a checklist of industry norms and expectations. Here are eight hiring philosophies that effective farm leaders follow.

- **Hire people you want to work with or who can teach you.** Co-workers spend hours, days, and weeks together. During any given week, the average worker will spend more time with their co-workers than with their families.

  Hiring best friends can lead to problems. Hiring these people creates an entourage, not a team. Entourages are fun but lack effectiveness. Teams are effective because they are productive, action-oriented, and sustainable.

Hiring someone you get along with is much better than hiring someone you don't like but who can do a task well. It is always easier to train a likable person to do a job than train an unlikeable person to be agreeable.

Farming is demanding work. Do not make it more difficult by making your workday miserable. You will dread work, resent coworkers, and eventually do or say something regrettable.

- **Hire people with positive attitudes.** Attitudes are both quintessential and contagious. Most small farms have only a few people working, and just one lousy mood can kill the team's energy and bring down morale. People will have an occasional off day, which is okay. A problem arises when that rare difficult day becomes the everyday norm.

  Attitudes guide actions. Once again, it is easier to train for skill or develop talent; it is nearly impossible to teach disposition. While attitudes occasionally change, small farmers have more pressing priorities than changing a person's perspective.

- **Hire people who get their hands dirty.** Remember, the smaller the farm, the more urgent the need for teamwork. There is no reason to hire a person who is unwilling to attempt a task. Not knowing how to do a job is both understandable and acceptable. Still, someone not willing to pitch in where needed is not suitable for any farm.

  It is the initiative to be a contributing team member. The best workers take charge and do something without being prompted. Equipment will break down, crops will not be ready for harvest, animals will get out, as well as a million other things. Whether rural or urban, small farms need people who are willing to adjust when the unexpected happens.

- **Hire capable people**. Everyone has potential, but not everyone is capable. Capable individuals have a particular disposition that allows them to attempt a task and to try new things. Disposition is a personality trait; one that is difficult to train, coach, or change.

- **Hire people positioned for professional growth**. You are more than your experience, and so are the people wanting to work with your farm. Potential is forward-looking; whereas, hiring on experience is backward-looking. Successful small farms focus on the future and not the past.

  Hiring for professional growth creates a productive workforce that is eager to grow. It is better to have a crew positioned for growth and lose people for opportunities elsewhere than keeping static people with no other job options.

- **Hire overqualified people.** Many hiring professionals say you should not hire overqualified people because they will leave when their situation improves. They are right, but so what?

  Very few businesses have lifetime employees. Besides, do you really want a lifetime employee in an entry-level position? A lifetime worker brings stagnation. Growing farms do not employ stagnant people; they employ growing people.

Overqualified people are value-added team players. Here's the deal. They are applying because they do not have other options, and most of these people will be excited you hired them. The best course of action is to be honest with them. Being honest with them encourages them to be honest with you.

Acknowledge they will be looking for a different job, but also work with them on that journey. The result will be a dedicated employee while employed and a future ambassador for your farm. Better yet, create a professional pathway for them with your farm.

- **Hire people that will complement your current team.** All teams have deficiencies. Leaders look for people who can fill in the gaps. Diversity improves teamwork while making the workplace more productive and enjoyable.

  Diversity is usually limited to superficial qualities such as race, nationality, gender, and other legally protected classes. These diversity elements are essential but not nearly as important as hiring people with diverse backgrounds, paradigms, and expertise.

- **Hire people that will open new markets or new networks**. Word of mouth advertising has always been the best form of small farm marketing. The more networks a farm connects with, the better the farm's position is for growth. It is tempting to hire someone because one of your best workers is friends with that person; however, will that hire improve your farm's marketing reach?

Hiring is critical for any small farm. Hiring the wrong person cannot only make you miserable but can potentially wipe out a season's worth of work. Take time when hiring, and do not just hire someone because you need a warm body for a day or two. Jim Collins said it this way, *"People are not your most important asset... the right people are."*

Training

> *"An organization's ability to learn, and translate that learning into action rapidly, is the ultimate competitive advantage."* ~ **Jack Welch**

Proper training ensures time and money spent on new talent is an investment, not an expense. It instills standards, practices, and processes, something that requires planning, diligence, and time. Because it communicates expectations and standards training, it is pivotal for small business success and a fundamental leadership task.

Too many people mistakenly believe training is simply showing or telling someone how to complete a task; it is not. Real training explains how to complete assignments correctly, be aware of cultural norms, and respect workplace expectations. Training or the lack of it also communicates importance.

Employee turnover is highest for new hires within the first two to four weeks of their initial start dates. This immediate turnover is the result of people feeling frustrated, confused, and abandoned. People are naturally nervous, anxious, and apprehensive when starting any new job. Carefully selected new team members are excited, desire to do well, and engaged. This "honeymoon phase" is the absolute best time to instill new skills, corporate values, and behaviors.

Training for skills and job tasks is essential, but training on culture, values, and behaviors is paramount. Impactful training begins by instilling corporate mission, values, and behaviors. This process builds a resilient organizational culture, which is a potent force. A farm's culture guides decisions and actions, good or bad. Developing a vigorous, dynamic, and productive environment comes from planning, implementation, and targeted interventions.

Once the new person understands the farm's culture, the training needs to switch to rudimentary items such as clocking in and out, pay periods, organizational structure, policies, procedures, etc. When training, there is nothing too basic to cover. Many small farms are great at overlooking little seemingly insignificant items; however, teaching these minor items communicates a small farm is a legitimate business.

Once people understand the culture, policies, and rules, shift the instruction to job-specific skills. Start with simple tasks before teaching complex tasks. Whether simple or complex, impactful training follows these eight steps.

- **Assessment.** There are two for proper evaluation. First, determine the target task or skill. When assessing a chore, identify the pivotal points and step sequence needed to complete the task correctly. Sometimes this is called job or task breakdown or analysis.

  Second, is the need to assess the trainee's prior knowledge or experience. People may have done a similar task before; however, this doesn't mean the job is done the same way or to the farm's expectation.

These assessments work to determine training needs. This assessment is the foundation of the training process as it identifies training needs, objectives, and plans.

- **Objectives**. Excellent training starts with clear objectives. Training objectives must guide instruction. The best targets are simple and easily understood. The goal is to explain the skill the trainee is learning without sounding pompous.

  Half the training and learning process is telling people what they are going to learn and why it is essential for their success. This understanding allows people to focus on skill acquisition and developing targeted questions instead of figuring out what is happening.

- **Training plan**. Plans, like objectives, must be concise while supporting the training objective. Let the task, goals, and objectives guide the program. For example, training to stack boxes in the back of a van requires a simple procedure; whereas, explaining how to test and adjust the pH level in a hydroponic system requires a more elaborate plan. Just remember the task determines the method.

- **Plan execution**. Better known as skill acquisition — the actual training. The best strategy is to show people what to do, have them do it, and then give feedback. Repeat this process until the task meets standards.

- **Evaluation and feedback**. Toastmasters International uses the sandwich technique, telling people what they did well, identifying growth opportunities, and providing the next steps. For maximum benefit, this process must be immediate and specific.

- **Fine-tuning**. People seldom develop a new skill set the first time. Providing people with an opportunity to learn, grow, and assimilate latest information is vital to their success. This fine-tuning takes time, practice, and patience.

- **Graduation**. Many businesses call the initial new hire period probation, which implies punishment. Having associates graduate from a training program creates a supportive work environment that acknowledges accomplishment.

- **Follow up**. Check back on the new hire to ensure the training stuck. It is better to do this sooner than later. Habits are easy to develop but difficult to change.

  It also shows people that you care, and they are valuable to the farm. Treat these follow-up sessions as informal pre-evaluation sessions. It reminds new associates what to focus on while clarifying expectations.

These training steps only work in environments that support, nurture, and encourage training. Leaders understand training is more than a checklist of steps; it is part of a farm's culture: its way of life.

Training succeeds because of productive relationships. The best hiring process offers only a superficial introduction to a new person. Productive workplace relationships need to be more than shallow; they must have substance, understanding, and mutual benefit. Training builds a more meaningful relationship with co-workers.

This relationship-building requires understanding people's motivation, drives, and goals. Conventional wisdom states company goals are the only thing that matters at work. That is wrong and outdated. It is misguided for two reasons. First, it creates an extremely one-sided relationship. Second, people have interests outside of work. Instead of wasting energy by fighting a losing battle that accelerates turnover, harness that energy by aligning individual motivation, drives, and goals with the farm's mission.

People learn better in safe environments that offer physical safety as well as emotional safety. Mistakes will happen. These mistakes are nothing more than learning opportunities that pinpoint the skills that need developing.

Providing a safe environment for learners diminishes anxiety. Anxiety brings with it two negative consequences. First, it impairs the learning process. Second, it depletes motivation. A safe learning environment creates a positive learning environment leading to better outcomes.

New jobs are stressful, and the new person is experiencing a personal transition. The role of a leader is to provide this person with support, encouragement, and reassurance. You will never regret encouraging someone in any situation, especially a new farm associate who wants to do well in their original position.

Coaching

Hiring and training is just the beginning. Continuous improvement and growth require constant coaching. **The objective of coaching is to develop individuals and teams to support growth through improved performance.** On a small farm, workplace coaching creates a loyal, productive, and engaged team: people working interdependently for a common goal.

All things equal, people do not quit jobs; people quit "leaders." When good people leave to take a similar position for equal pay in the same setting, there is a leadership problem. When good people move on for a promotion with more income, there is authentic leadership. There are four essential coaching assumptions.

- **People have potential.** Everyone has the capacity for growth, improvement, and learning. The goal of a coach is to facilitate this positive change.

- **Feedback is essential.** People must understand how and what to improve. Feedback is as much about listening as it is about talking. Listening leads to an increased understanding of what trainees need to know.

- **Supportive workplace.** People need professional support to reach career goals. People are social creatures designed to work in groups.

- **Growth mindset**. People want to grow, and if a person does not want to grow, replace them with someone who does.

Coaching is effective when implemented correctly.

To begin the coaching process, there are eight coaching practices to follow.

1. **Formal feedback**. People need feedback on their work performance. Farming supplies many opportunities to speak harshly to someone, especially when the cows or pigs have escaped. These events must not be the only time an employee receives feedback; if it were, it would be easy for that person to think they are not valued.

   Regular formal feedback allows employees to get a complete picture of their performance. Employee feedback is mandatory for individual and organizational development, which is why it has its own section.

2. **Listening**. Associates are a reliable source of information. Listening to employees is one of the absolute best ways to communicate; they are valuable members of a farm's community.

3. **Culturally embedded**. There are reasons large businesses focus on organizational culture. It is because culture guides behavior, shapes attitudes, and communicates expectations. When coaching is embedded in the culture, people are more engaged in the coaching process, creating better results.

4. **Milestones**. Create certificates to acknowledge milestones and accomplishments. This is a low-cost

high-result motivational tool that encourages achievement. People like recognition. This provides a solid record of progress while creating career pathways.

5. **Create pathways.** People need direction, hope, and vision. Career paths meet these needs in an obvious tangible way. Not only that but also, this taps into the most potent free-market force: the pursuit of individual self-interest.

   When people's personal interests and workplace interests are aligned, work performance and farm loyalty multiply. Leaders understand this and work to make this connection as it is a true win-win.

6. **Develop employee efficacy**. This is the intersection of self-belief and competence. Increased employee efficacy improves task delegation. Leaders who want control over their schedules, days off, or task choices must employ dependable people.

7. **Keep it personal**. Provide specific and individualized feedback. Don't share what you said to this person with other associates. We all need to feel valued, respected, and supported. Personal and targeted feedback does that.

8. **Keep it professional**. Don't attack a person's personality. Talk in terms of performance and behavior.

Mentoring

Mentoring is a central leadership task. This book approaches farm mentoring as a process of creating farm leaders. This process shares beliefs, wisdom, and experience through a formal relationship designed to grow people. The objective is to prepare individuals for their next career step, which, in this case, is a leadership role in farming.

Mentorships differ from internships. Many small farms use internships as nothing more than an attempt to source free labor, which is unfair and unproductive. It is unjust to individuals seeking skills, experience, and expertise. It is fruitless for the farm. It wastes resources while exploiting people for marginal benefits when the farm could have invested those resources into actual growth activities.

Legally speaking, internships are short-term assignments for potential employees. If there is not a possible career position after the internship, it is not an internship! It is unpaid or underpaid labor, which may create problems if a state's labor department investigates the farm's labor practices.

The primary difference between mentorships and internships is mentorships develop more profound, more meaningful relationships; whereas, internships keep relationships at the superficial level. The most critical difference is farm mentorships create leaders; whereas, farm internships create entry-level workers.

Mentoring differs from coaching. Mentoring develops the person; coaching develops talent, skill sets, or both. Mentoring differs from training; training develops a job-specific skill or task mastery. Growing businesses, especially small farms, need mentoring, coaching, and training.

Farm mentorships are vital to the revitalization of small farms, urban market gardens, and rural economic development. The problems faced by these indispensable sectors can be solved when optimistic visionary leaders build human capital. Besides, having quality people working with you is much better than a workforce of idiots working against you. There are six mentorship benefits.

1. **Mentorships allow farm leaders to reflect and redefine their practices.** Mentoring requires reflection, which is an intentional and deliberate analysis of beliefs, actions, and procedures.

2. **Mentorships allow farms to be recognized as industry and community leaders.** It never hurts to be an industry leader. This position allows for greater visibility and opportunities. Industry leaders attract skillful workers and more faithful customers.

3. **Mentorships create fresh marketing opportunities.** Mentees can be an entry point into a new market or help develop a new product line. Either way, new marketing opportunities exist for the farm.

4. **Mentorships create a healthier more productive small farm culture.** A properly developed and implemented mentoring program is an extension of a farm's culture. Strong organizational cultures

are clearly defined, developed, and supported. A formal mentor program instills corporate values, beliefs, and behaviors in inspiring leaders.

5. **Mentorships can create a foundation for future partnerships.** There is a limit to what one person can do. Having quality, dependable, and capable people able to assist in growth activities is essential for sustainability. It includes having people help with tasks such as product or market development. These people afford you the freedom to spend time on the aspects of farming you most enjoy.

6. **Mentorships are an investment in your farm, community, and industry.** Human capital is the only creative resource, which means investing in people is one of the most profitable investment decisions.

Effective mentor programs don't happen. They are the result of intentional planning, development, and execution. There are nine guidelines to follow.

1. **Role clarification.** People must know what role they are playing and why. Granted, every associate requires training and coaching; however, not every worker requires mentoring. Everyone has potential, ability, and the capacity to lead; however, not everyone desires to do more, be more, or to lead others.

    The best mentor programs are selective and only work with people with a growth mindset, who strive for excellence, and who have a passion for farming. It is especially true when the mentor program's goal is to develop farm leaders willing and eager to assume a leadership position with your farm.

Mentoring is not limited to members of your farm. You can mentor other farmers as well. When mentoring other farmers, I recommend a formal agreement; otherwise, the relationship will become muddled and complicated, and you will become frustrated.

2. **Accountability**. The mentor and mentee need to be accountable to each other. By definition, a mentor is a wise trusted counselor and a role model, and the mentee must be a willing and eager participant desiring personal and professional growth.

    Accountability is not punitive. It is about meeting a set of predetermined standards based on values, culture, and mission. Accountability works best when growth is the target, and people have autonomy and ownership of the process.

3. **Strategy**. Mentor programs must align with business strategy; otherwise, it becomes a distraction and just another to-do. Small farms either grow or die, and mentor programs must support growth.

4. **Goals and objectives**. What is the desired result of the mentor program? Is the mentee going to be promoted? Will the mentee leave the farm and start their own farm? Will they improve their existing farm? Without a clear and precise goal or aim, mentor programs are ineffective.

5. **Assessment and feedback**. There needs to be an understanding of what learning needs to happen

and why it is essential. This assessment must support the program's objectives; the result is a workable plan of action for people to follow.

6. **Planning.** The mentee's need is the basis of the plan. A common mistake is implementing a one-size-fits-all approach to the mentoring process, which is a frustrating method.

   Mentoring develops leaders who are going to move up or on. Treating people as individuals, not cogs in a machine, is the only way to accomplish this goal. Planning connects all parties in a meaningful way by ensuring the meeting of emotional, learning, and growth needs. Most importantly, this process creates a framework that communicates expectations, education, and outcomes.

7. **Execution.** Mentoring is a formal process. Its implementation starts with a meeting discussing learning and progress toward learning targets. The meeting could be weekly, bi-weekly, or monthly. While there is not a magic number of meeting frequency, the meeting times must be consistent.

8. **Fine-tuning.** Things change, and so will the plan. That doesn't mean anything was necessarily wrong with the original idea. It just means that new facts and opportunities emerged.

9. **Exit point.** Mentoring is not a lifetime commitment. In all great stories, the protagonist must go it alone on his or her quest. The same is true for your mentee. When people complete the program's goals and objectives, set them free.

Mentor programs, unlike training and coaching, can be open to non-employees. Small farm leaders are free to mentor other small farmers. It requires an investment of time, which explains the need for a reasonable fee. There is no need to gouge people; however, all farms have endless chores. If the leader is not doing these chores, someone else is.

More importantly, people express value by what they pay for. Charging non-employees is the best way to get people to treat the process seriously as an investment.

Providing feedback

> *"By creating a feedback culture within your office, you ensure that people continue to learn, grow, and challenge themselves."* ~ **Neil Blumenthal**

Leaders are continually giving feedback, whether they realize it or not. A cliché warns people to think before speaking. It is especially true for leaders because leaders' words can motivate, encourage, and inspire people or demoralize, discourage, and shut down effort.

Feedback must be growth-centered. Positive informal feedback is one of the best methods for improving overall farm performance. Tom Rath states that *"Employees who report receiving recognition and praise within the last seven days show increased productivity, get higher scores from customers, and have better safety records. They're just more engaged at work."*

Feedback comes in two varieties: informal and formal. Anytime a leader comments regarding performance or behavior outside of a formal evaluation, it is informal. This reason is why informal feedback is the most common and valuable form of feedback.

Formal feedback is limited in scope and has an essential role in semi-annual or annual performance reviews. It creates an official record of performance, establishes new benchmarks, and lets people know where they stand. Informal feedback, on the other hand, is continuous and given without limitations.

Written mission statements, core values, and policies are needed when communicating expectations to associates. More persuasive than well-crafted and formal documents is the feedback people received from leaders. Feedback, especially informal feedback, relates what is truly meaningful to the farm.

There are eight best practices for giving feedback.

1. **Be specific**. While there is nothing wrong with a general attaboy such as "good job," it lacks breadth depth of purpose. Specifics such as, *"I like the way you stayed calm with that rude customer today."* Or, *"When the trailer tire caught on fire, you did a great job staying calm while getting the fire extinguisher."*

2. **Performance and mission alignment.** Feedback needs to align with the farm's purpose and mission. Providing this specific feedback is a terrific way to restate the farm's purpose while reinforcing its culture.

3. **Timely.** The best feedback is always immediate. Some instances require a cooling-down period; however, the general rule of thumb is immediate feedback is the best feedback.

4. **Praise in public.** Genuinely praising someone is a convincing cultural event. It is a visible and powerful communication strategy that clearly emphasizes priorities.

5. **Critique in private.** When someone screws up, don't make the situation worse by embarrassing the offending staff member. Embarrassing people only intensifies a problem while not offering a solution. It causes two problems. First, it creates resentment. Second, it unnecessarily escalates an already tense situation.

   Lastly, it ignores significant facts that may arise when discussing the situation in private. Leaders make better decisions with all the information and are not merely reacting to a headline like people do when arguing on social media.

6. **Performance over personality.** It is vital for a great reason. Some people are amicable, fun, and even super cool to be around but are horrible workers. The latter offers only distractions instead of results. On the other hand, some people lack social skills but are great at their job. Focus on what is essential for their role on the farm as feedback is provided.

7. **Separate problems from symptoms.** Employees only have so much control over things, just as you only have so much control over things. Be sure feedback is limited to what the employee controls.

8. **Actionable.** Feedback should help the employees improve workplace performance. Feedback allows people to recognize preferred actions or make better decisions given their current position and sphere of influence. Always ensure any

recommended actions or behaviors are within the employee's control.

Terminating employees

Some people must go. This harsh reality happens for many reasons, including people who do not fit into a farm's culture. This group drains energy while sowing discontent among team members. Some people will also not complete the required tasks or will refuse to complete assignments to standards. Once again, anyone in that group of people needs to go.

Whether a person is not a fit organizationally or lacks the skills to do the job, termination should never be a surprise — especially to the person losing their job. The hiring process, when done correctly, clearly communicates the farm's culture and performance expectations. Proper training provides resources and tools to perform according to standards. Coaching and feedback provide opportunities to refine skills, adjust behaviors, and adopt new attitudes.

When these things do not work, it is in everyone's best interest to terminate the employee. It is not fair to employ someone in a position for which they are not suited. When leaders do their job correctly, employees know when they are failing, and keeping people hanging on unnecessarily is a disservice to them and the farm.

Terminating employees requires care, concern, and consideration. It benefits all parties involved. It helps you because people are watching, allowing staff members to examine your character and ethics. Terminating employees is a very public display of integrity, even when handled quietly and discretely.

It benefits the employee as it allows them to maintain dignity and respect. There is a significant chance that the dismissed employee will maintain personal relationships with one or more of your current employees. These people will talk no matter what you do or say to discourage it.

When these people socialize, you do not want them talking about the "jackass way" you let someone go. You want people saying that you did everything you could do to save that person's job. You want the person you fired to defend you on their firing, which can happen.

There is no amount of saying *"business is business"* or *"just doing my job"* that will satisfy or reassure remaining employees. Associates need to know they are supported, and the actions taken when terminating a person communicate volumes. It highlights an important distinction between leadership and management. Leaders understand the full impact of their decisions; whereas, managers follow policy and back up poor decisions by hiding behind the words, *"It's just policy."* Remember, small farm leaders never hide behind corporate policy and procedures. Here are the 10 best practices for terminating employees.

1. **Communicate.** Let people know in advance what they are doing right and what needs improvement. People need to know when their job is in jeopardy and what they can do to save it. Most people find not having an income is a great motivator. If this doesn't motivate them, it is a sign they do not want to continue employment with your farm but lack the willingness to leave voluntarily.

2. **New roles.** The underperforming employee may be in the wrong position. If a person lives the farm's values and mission, give them a chance to test new or dissimilar roles before replacing them. These people, like everyone else, excel and fail at various things.

3. **Give warnings.** Feedback may need to include clear signals if people are not performing. Helpful feedback provides critical information as well as praise. This conversation must have an improvement or an exit plan.

4. **Document.** Terminating employees provides an opportunity for legal liability. Avoiding lawsuits is as simple as recording and documenting employee conversations. Written warnings paired with correction plans tend to be ample evidence the employee dismissal was fair and legal.

5. **Provide an out.** Give people opportunities to volunteer to leave. It is better if they go on their own than firing them. One method of this includes reducing their hours or assigning undesirable shifts or tasks until performance improves.

6. **Performance-based compensation.** Many farm positions are hourly positions. Paying by the hour is a straightforward way of rewarding higher performers with more hours. It is fair and equitable because it allows more valuable employees to earn more money. It also benefits the lower performers as well. With reduced hours, they still have a paycheck with an opportunity to improve skills or seek employment elsewhere. As a side note, piece work or performance pay fits well in this model.

Performance-based scheduling improves overall farm efficiency. It is true if expectations are clear, and all associates have equal access to tools and learning resources.

7. **Review documentation.** During coaching and feedback sessions, review previous documentation, including the clearly outlined "next steps" discussed during prior meetings. It should lead to one of two outcomes: improved performance or termination. Either way, the associate is accountable.

8. **Transfer accountability.** Review documentation, and ask the employee what they would do if they were in charge. Almost always, the person agrees termination is warranted. Using their recommendation is a fantastic way to avoid lawsuits and to maintain workplace morale.

9. **Listen.** Listening doesn't mean agreement. It means understanding that person's point of view. The goal is to show empathy for someone who just lost a job.

10. **Be firm.** By thoroughly training, coaching, and providing feedback, leaders have done their job. In most cases, leaders have gone above and beyond what is required. People deserve second chances; however, at this point, opportunities have been exhausted.

Weeding is vital for both the garden and the organizational culture. Terminating employees is a weeding out process. Think of it as creating and supporting a proper environment for growth. Lastly, never jeopardize your business for someone who doesn't care enough about your business to meet minimum standards.

Grow Community

*"Culture is simply a shared way of doing something with a passion." ~ **Brian Chesky***

Your farm is part of a community, as well as its own community. It is okay if a farm to not "fit in" with the local community or neighbors. Visionary leaders are often laughed at, ridiculed, and mocked for ideas and actions.

Friends and neighbors are not responsible, nor will they be held liable for your success or failures. Just as you are not responsible or accountable for your neighbors' success or failure. Your primary responsibility is to the success of your farm, and you only have a limited secondary obligation (at best) to your neighbors.

The absolute best action any small farmer can do for their community is to be extraordinarily successful. This leadership form is more valuable to struggling communities than any policy brought forth by an elected official or any program implemented by a non-profit organization.

The more money and visitors you bring into your community, the better for all. This actualizes the aphorism, *"a rising tide lifts all boats."* This breeds competition, and competition builds economies while bringing out the best in the community.

Also, the more successful a farm, the better relationships it can have with all stakeholders. Effective relationships flourish when people are interdependent. To be interdependent people, however, people and organizations must be independent. If the parties are not independent in every sense of the word, codependent relationships emerge. Codependent relationships always benefit the person with the most power at the expense of the weaker party.

The problem for the stronger party is they become complacent. Content people quickly become smug and self-serving while failing to actualize their fullest potential. Benjamin E. Mays said it this way, "*The tragedy of life is often not in our failure, but rather in our complacency; not in our doing too much, but rather in our doing too little; not in our living above our ability, but rather in our living below our capacities.*"

Small farms are communities. By definition, a community has structure, norms, and values. These elements are the foundation of a farm's social identity.

One of the greatest opportunities in the small or family farm world is to reconnect people with the wonder of nature and the sacrifice required of life. Doing this requires small farm leaders with vision and understanding of the importance and role of organizational culture.

A century ago, farms were gathering places. People would visit family for the holidays or weekends, and they were places to create family memories. Today, people are removed from rural America. They are detached from food production, the land, and the wonders of rural America.

Organizational culture

"I used to believe that culture was 'soft,' and had little bearing on our bottom line. What I believe today is that our culture has everything to do with our bottom line, now and into the future."

~ **Vern Dosch**

Soil offers the best example of organizational culture. It is living, comprised of microbes, minerals, and moisture. What makes soil productive is what is below the surface, what we don't see. Over time soil changes, and just like soil, organizational culture lives and evolves. Culture begins with any human interaction. Corporate culture requires mission, purpose, and values for its foundation and human behavior for its structure.

Healthy soil is the foundation of thriving farms. Healthy soil supports and sustains thriving ecosystems, and without hardy soil, nothing good grows. The importance of soil is evident to many farmers; however, organizational culture's power is not apparent to enough farmers.

There are several reasons for this. First, many practical task-driven small farmers believe culture is just fluff or touchy-feely nonsense. It is not. Corporate culture brings human emotions, desires, and hopes into the farm business. Additionally, building culture reduces isolation and depression, two common mental problems faced by many small farmers.

Second, many people mistakenly think this works only for large organizations. All groups have a culture, whether it is intentionally defined or not. A small farm is a substantial individual investment of time and money. Resources that must yield a profit while developing a strong culture is no guarantee of success, but its absence promises failure.

Third, many people do not understand the complexities of developing culture. Culture, like soil, has many components and working parts. Each input needs analysis to determine how it will interact with other parts of the system.

Finally, many people don't believe it is crucial, which is an enormous and expensive mistake. It is the farm's way of life and the expression of self-selected standards, purposes, and philosophies. Culture manifests hopes, dreams, and desires. In short, culture breathes life into the farm dream.

Just as farmers test their soil and make adjustments, a farm's culture needs testing and modification. Rich culture, like healthy soil, brings forth life and abundance. It is a life force that allows people to pursue a common purpose with passion, pride, and persistence.

Why is it important? Your farm is where you live your dream. Without a vigorous corporate culture, employees view work as just a job, devoid of meaning and attachment. With a healthy culture, people experience work as meaningful, fulfilling a purpose, and building a career.

All businesses have a unique style of working. Small farms are no different, and this style of work builds culture. Beliefs, philosophies, principles, and values shape a farm's work style. A winning culture provides the following nine benefits for small farms.

1. **Communication.** Culture communicates what a farm stands for to people inside and outside of your farm. Culture expresses meaning, which is the

essence of communication. Steadfast cultures increase shared purpose and understanding of organizational objectives.

2. **Competition**. Small farms compete in many ways. Culture improves competitive efficacy. Large retailers can easily outspend small farms on marketing, processes, and operational efficiencies. A strong culture is a farm's best defense against industry titans seeking to destroy small farms and rural America.

   The Battle of Thermopylae is a prime example of the importance of culture. The Spartan culture gave strength to the 300 Spartans, who fought a much larger Persian army. Small farmers have the same odds fighting against large businesses as the Spartans had against the Persians. Still, just as the Spartans eventually stopped the Persian invasion, small farmers can stop the onslaught of attacks from mega-corporations.

3. **Brand image**. Culture provides a framework for storytelling and sharing a small farm's brand with others. Branding is the most crucial tool that farmers possess for business building; however, brands don't just happen. Brands are grown, developed, and refined the same way as culture is cultivated, developed, and refined.

   Attractive brands are an extension of an organization's culture. If there is no alignment between branding and culture, customers will be disappointed, and associates will be disgruntled.

4. **Identity.** A farm's corporate identity is nothing more than its self-image. As with people, corporate

self-image requires managing, and just as people need a positive healthy self-image, so does a business.

A farm's identity creates a platform to share a common purpose while creating a place where people belong. Also, it is the basis for effective branding. Strong brands build sustainable businesses, which is why large corporations invest heavily in culture and branding activities.

5. **Advocates.** Compelling culture transforms people into advocates for your small farm. Purposeful culture provides a sense of ownership for employees, which increases workplace commitment. Doug Conant said it this way, *"To win in the marketplace, you must first win in the workplace."*

   Employees are good farm advocates, but customers are the best farm advocates. The best form of advertising will always be word of mouth; however, people need a compelling reason to promote your farm to acquaintances. Quality products are the first step, followed by a purpose people can rally behind.

6. **Retention.** An influential culture creates a sense of belonging. All things equal, people remain with an employer who values them. Some people will even turn down a promotion or higher wage from competing employers to stay valued.

   Don't get me wrong, money is irreplaceable, and people deserve a fair wage for the position. People also deserve an emotionally rewarding place to work. A common misconception is that a workplace can either be a "good" place to work or pay well, but the reality is that a business can be both.

7. **Reduces friction.** People work better when they are on the same page. A well-defined culture creates a shared purpose and experience. Also, it provides a common language, values, and behaviors. Many workplace conflicts are the result of misaligned or ambiguous goals and objectives.

   Reducing friction requires a workplace with clearly communicated vision, mission, and values, along with specific clearly defined behaviors. These elements become a framework for accountability, ownership, and communication. It ensures when things go wrong, people will be able to separate symptoms from problems.

8. **Provides predictability.** People must be able to anticipate responses to various situations. An influential culture allows people to make better decisions, judgments, and choices. People need predictability in their lives, especially their jobs.

   Predictability creates consistency. Repeat customers happen because they liked what happened previously. Product or service consistency only happens when small farms have a positive culture, one that guides employees to do the right thing for customers at the right time.

9. **Actualizes purpose.** Culture is nothing more than living a small farm's mission, vision, and values. This book talks much about purpose and passion for a reason. A farm offers an opportunity for people to live a life of their design. Creating a well-

defined farm culture turns that dream into reality while keeping that dream from becoming a nightmare.

Building strong culture

> "Organizational Culture is the 'water' in the fishbowl. If the water is clean, nourishing, energizing the fish will thrive and if the water is toxic the fish will die..."
> ~ **Ranjan De Silva**

Organizational culture starts and ends with leadership. The great thing about owning a small farm is you develop the culture according to your design. Many consultants, experts, and authors talk about employee "buy-in" and giving people a voice when creating culture. That sounds nice as part of a well-rehearsed speech. However, it is your farm, dream, and passion; therefore, your voice is the most critical.

We all have had jobs that we loved and jobs we found tormenting. Some of us have enjoyed working somewhere while disliking the position, industry, or tasks. On the other hand, we all have jobs where we loved the work but hated the workplace. The reason for either situation is work-place culture.

Culture building is the most crucial leadership function for any business that employs people. A robust culture instills a sense of pride, purpose, and passion in the workplace. Here are the six "D"s of organization culture.

1. **Define it**. Clearly define the culture. It starts with mission and vision statements, workplace values, and expected behaviors. Next, leaders must explain

the farm's beliefs and philosophies, which becomes the driving force behind the business strategy.

This step communicates work-place expectations to associates. When training people, this is as important as task mastery. Having competent people who embody culture allows leaders freedom and flexibility. It also reduces leadership stress because leaders no longer need to worry about workers meeting standards because they know standards are met.

2. **Design it**. Culture turns lofty-sounding statements into real-world action. Job tasks and responsibilities must support culture. Any misalignment creates confusion, weakens culture, and breeds unnecessary conflict.

    Workplace rewards and compensation must align with the culture, including scheduling, task assignments, and promotions. A common mistake is to promote people on performance while ignoring their lack of regard for farm values or for disregarding **your** principles.

3. **Deliver it**. The first two steps are easy, but this step is where the rubber meets the road. Recently, I had a conversation with a farmer who was complaining about a difficult worker.

    This farmer reasoned it made good business sense to keep this guy. The farmer's rationale was at the end of the day, the troubled employee brought in more money than the farmer spent on him. As a result, the farmer didn't think it would be a good idea to fire this person.

I disagree for three reasons. First, values are not for sale. Keeping a person who doesn't live organizational values for a few dollars cheapens values. More importantly, keeping this person is a clear signal of a lack of integrity, dependability, and conviction. In other words, it a sign of weak leadership.

Secondly, it brings down staff morale, creates conflict, and compromises integrity. These things consistently lower productivity, albeit indirectly. These indirect costs are usually much higher than the extra dollar or two gained from allowing a so-called performer to remain.

Third, this gives too much power to someone who doesn't respect you; it transfers power, control, and influence to a saboteur. While people are not replaceable, a person is. Many people want to work on a small farm. Granted, these people may be out of your current area, but the internet makes these people reachable. People are looking for work with the same passions as you and who would be happy to join your farm's pursuit of its mission.

4. **Develop people.** It is the purpose of training, coaching, and mentoring. Effective farm-training programs build and sustain culture. It is also much better to hire people who already support and live corporate values and train them to do a particular task than to teach a mindset.

5. **Develop feedback loops.** Culture is a function of communication. Feedback loops explain the cause and effect of culture. People need to know how they fit into the culture as well as the required adjustments.

Feedback loops allow for self-correction. People are more prone to change their behavior when it comes from within. Besides, feedback loops are a mechanism for peers to provide performance feedback; however, this only works if there is a universal language paired with clear expectations.

6. **Dispatch obstacles.** Some people are never going to match a farm's culture. There is no reason a person should interfere with another person's performance, no matter how great a person is at a particular task.

   Just as gardeners cull plants and pull weeds, the same process should happen with people. Some highly competent people will choke out soon-to-be-great people who live your farm's values. Managers keep highly skilled people because they can get the job done; whereas, leaders weed those folks out, so other people can become more productive.

Culture is a farm's personality, as well as a reason to bond with the farm in an intensely loyal way. Businesses such as Starbucks, Chick-fil-A, Southwest Airlines, and Waffle House are cultural icons because they understand culture's power. It is no accident that these companies and many other businesses use organizational culture as a strategic business tool.

Develop a loyal following

> *"Make your customer the hero of your story."*
> ~ Ann Handley

Culture is the expression of a farm's values, emotions, and behaviors. Culture is the farm's corporate personality

— its identity. Culture makes a farm unique while guiding branding, marketing, and business decisions.

For customers, culture communicates quality products and services. Profitable farm culture creates purposeful customer service while building a strong farm reputation. A strong culture creates repeat customers, who transform into farm advocates. Productive farm culture establishes an emotional appeal, makes a connection, and gives a human touch to a farm. In short, farm culture is its personality and voice.

Small farms are perfect places for building a loyal following. People want to know their food's source. Also, nostalgia is a powerful emotion. Small farm leaders who understand the power of culture and nostalgia have an advantage. The reason is small farms are not only a special place to raise children but also a place for other people to create memories with their children. Building a following takes time, purpose, and intentionality. Here are eight practices to develop your farm's following.

1. **Quality.** Nothing builds a business better than quality products and services. Leaders must invest and develop excellent products, practices, and processes. When leaders focus on superiority, they are investing in and securing a profitable future.

    Quality is a way of life for sustainable businesses, and it communicates caring, pride, and passion. Leaders understand products brought to market reflect who they are and what they stand for.

2. **Story**. People love stories and buy into larger-than-life narratives. For example, Chick-fil-A and Hobby Lobby are closed on Sundays, creating a narrative

that reflects their stated values and appealing to their customers' spiritual needs and sensibilities.

It is tempting to copy the stories of others — don't. Plagiarized stories are dull, boring, and cliché; whereas, original stories are compelling, exciting, and powerful.

3. **Authenticity**. It is a core leadership trait. Being authentic in a fake world creates a standout. There is no need to be something you are not. Being authentic requires nothing more than living your values. Andie MacDowell puts it this way, *"When you are authentic, you create a certain energy, people want to be around you because you are unique."*

Authenticity attracts loyal customers, builds goodwill with suppliers, and brings out the best in employees. People can and will copy a farm's products and practices, but they cannot copy authenticity.

4. **Passion**. It is galvanizing when shared; sharing requires answering two questions. First, why do you farm? Second, what intrinsic rewards do you get from farming? When answering these questions, do not give a superficial answer. Instead, provide a deeply emotional and spiritual response (even if people laugh at you).

Avoid answering these questions with the bland, boring, and wrong answer, *"to pay the bills."* It commoditizes farm products, minimizes farmer worth, insults passionate farmers, and drives customers and employees away. It is the least motivating and most damaging response possible. If this is your answer, rethink your career choices.

5. **Develop a voice**. A farm's voice expresses its personality, values, and beliefs. It tells the farm's story while communicating its "why" or the reasons guiding actions. Farming is hard work and is a challenging industry to earn a profit. Selling commodities makes profitability difficult, especially for small-scale farmers.

   A clear message connects a farm with people with similar values, hopes, and dreams. Also, a farm's voice must be consistent, on-target, and precise. The only way for this to happen is to speak from the heart.

6. **Value-driven**. Value in this context includes two equally essential meanings. First, it is what the small farm stands for and believes in — the farm's ethics. Second, it requires creating customer value. Customers keep a farm in business, but living values and ethics make life rewarding.

   Non-price sensitive people follow value-driven brands. This group of customers is the most profitable group of customers for any small farm. Many farmers scoff, mock, and ridicule these people and describe them as tree-hugging hippies, which is a mistake. Small farmers should embrace this valued driven group of people who are price insensitive.

   Small farmers who are eager to help these people actualize their values will gain a loyal customer base. It has always been a good business idea to provide customers the products and services they want, and these customers have clearly stated product preferences.

7. **Engagement**. Get people involved in your farm. Invite people out for events, offer tours, and have an active presence on social media. By letting people into your farm's world, you are becoming a part of their world. This engagement creates bonds, loyal customers, and employees.

   People can get food anywhere. However, people will not feel connected to their local mega-store or chain restaurant. If given the opportunity, they will become connected with your farm if you create opportunities and build community with them.

8. **Relationships**. Sustainable small farms form solid relationships with customers and employees. Today more than ever, people are looking for locally sourced products and relationships with farmers. Take advantage of this opportunity by being open and ready to build relationships.

   The current trend is to buy locally; however, people prefer to buy from a caring person. More importantly, people are willing to spend extra money when there is a relationship. Relationships are the foundation of community. These relationships create more than customers and employees; they form friendships that last a lifetime and recruit farm advocates.

Creating a farm community is excellent for business. It positions the farm as a community leader, creates brand value, and builds a sustainable business. Small farm and rural economic revitalization depend on leaders willing to build communities.

Grow a Farm Legacy

"Legacy is not leaving something for people, it's leaving something in people." ~ **Peter Strople**

Don't build a farm; build a legacy. The foundation of legacy is building a farm on the qualities you desire to instill in your children and grandchildren. These qualities are more than what people are going to talk about during your funeral. These qualities are going to create stories shared with generations. Legacy allows you to influence people you will never meet.

People need to connect. People have a desire to bond with each other, nature, and the universe. A small farm is a great way to meet these very human needs. Building a sustainable small farm that contributes to society creates a legacy. Small farms are one of the few places left that allow people to transform a vocation into a legacy: a life lesson for future generations.

Why do you farm?

"A master in the art of living draws no sharp distinction between his work and his play; his labor and his leisure..."
~ **Lawrence Pearsall Jacks**

Whether it is a few hundred acres in a rural area or less than an acre in an urban environment, a farm is an individual dream. Building a farm's legacy requires purpose. Buddha said, *"Your purpose in life is to find your purpose and give your whole heart and soul to it."*

Granted, a farm can survive with the mundane purpose of growing and selling food. This unassuming existence is not motivating for the next generation. This can create generational resentment because new generations are toiling without purpose, direction, or acceptance.

Farming with purpose, pride, and passion creates a legacy: generational pride. This pride provides life lessons for future generations. It builds a family who cares about each other, fights for each other, and supports each other. Small farms are one of the few remaining places that nurture this pursuit. Having a farm allows people to craft family history while giving future generations a sense of belonging, clear expectations, and living standards.

Small farmers are unique in that there is no distinction between work, family, and leisure. Even when a small farmer is not physically working, he or she is thinking about the farm. Even on vacation, the farmer's mind, heart, and soul is at the farm while the body is miles away.

Create something that matters

> *"No matter how small you start, start something that matters."* ~ **Brendon Burchard**

People will think you are crazy when you tell them you are building a farm that matters. That's their problem. Too many people use fear, uncertainty, and limiting beliefs as a compass for life choices. Those people are not leaders; they are followers. Farm leaders are unique. They strive to create something significant built on carefully selected values, principles, and beliefs.

The search for meaning brought humans from the wilderness to the stone age and then to the technological age. This search led people to all parts of the world. It built modern civilization. The drive behind this search can allow the smallest farm to grow into a sustainable enterprise, one that can make a difference for its community and the world.

Personally speaking, I love small farms because they are one of the few businesses that include all family members to varying degrees. I am not saying that kids or spouses need to be employed full-time by the farm. The fact is they can contribute, and be involved physically and emotionally with a farm while pursuing their dreams. Small farms offer many opportunities for family members to connect in various meaningful ways at multiple levels.

Creating something that matters starts with the leader. Leaders must not only love their business, but also they must share that love with others. Small farm leaders must be devoted, passionate, and believe in their practices, processes, and products.

Successful small farming and legacy building require new ways of thinking and acting. Also, it will require new and innovative takes on farm products and services. It requires new rules. Submitting to industry norms solidifies a business as an industry follower and not as an industry leader. Antiquated industry norms or expectations do not bind visionary farm leaders. Innovative farm leaders develop a unique voice and champion their own causes.

Creating a legacy is really about living life to the fullest. Umair Haque states, "*You have one job. And that is to live an extraordinary life...*" Creating a legacy serves as an example of accomplishment while inspiring others to create greatness for themselves. Set larger-than-life goals. As you accomplish those goals, you become an inspiration for others, including your offspring. **If you do that, I promise you will grow your own way.**

22 Leadership Principles

1. Leaders lead themselves before leading others.

2. Leaders know how to follow.

3. Leaders are customer-driven and strive to develop products, processes, and practices that meet customer needs.

4. Leaders have vision.

5. Leaders are driven by a sense of mission.

6. Leaders use principle-based values to guide decisions and behaviors.

7. Leaders understand that people follow people, not positions.

8. Leaders are curious and driven to learn as much as they can.

9. Leaders have high but realistic standards.

10. Leaders strive for excellence and not perfection.

11. Leaders have a bias for action.

12. Leaders think deeply and avoid the superficial.

13. Leaders think big, have a dream, and utilize strategy.

14. Leaders embrace the full range of human emotions.

15. Leaders care about their communities.

16. Leaders inspire through passion, commitment, and purpose.

17. Leaders have gumption.

18. Leaders have conviction and are willing to challenge the status quo.

19. Leaders build trust through consistency.

20. Leaders are long-term thinkers.

21. Leaders grow others.

22. Leaders lead.

Useful Quotes

"The two most important days in your life are the day you are born and the day you find out why." ~ **Mark Twain**

"Tradition becomes our security, and when the mind is secure it is in decay." ~ **Jiddu Krishnamurti**

"To handle yourself, use your head; to handle others, use your heart." ~ **Eleanor Roosevelt**

"Our chief want is someone who will inspire us to be what we know we could be." ~ **Ralph Waldo Emerson**

"If your actions create a legacy that inspires others to dream more, learn more, do more and become more, then you are an excellent leader." ~ **Dolly Parton**

"What you stay focused on will grow." ~ Roy T. Bennett

"There is nothing in a caterpillar that tells you it's going to be a butterfly. "~ **Buckminster Fuller**

"The secret of leadership is simple: Do what you believe in. Paint a picture of the future. Go there. People will follow." ~ **Seth Godin**

"If you are working on something that you really care about, you don't have to be pushed. The vision pulls you." ~ **Steve Jobs**

*"Creativity Is Intelligence Having Fun.**"** – Albert Einstein*

"Motivation is what gets you started. Habit is what keeps you going." ~ **Jim Ryun**

"*Your vision will become clear only when you look into your heart. Who looks outside, dreams; who looks inside, awakes.*" ~ **Carl Jung**

"*Whatever you can do or dream you can, begin it. Boldness has genius, and magic and power in it. Begin it now.*" ~ **Goethe**

"*When entire companies embrace a growth mindset, their employees report feeling far more empowered and committed; they also receive far greater organizational support for collaboration and innovation.*" ~ **Carol S. Dweck**

"*The basic skills of leaders are always the same: be driven by a deeper purpose, be a human being, have a passion for what you do, and it's also about hard work and ethics.*" ~ **Paul Polman**

"*Developing people is more important than developing practices and processes.*" ~ **Jason McClure**

"*Ignore others, forget about the competition, and focus on living your dreams and grow your own way.*" ~ **Jason McClure**

Available on Amazon

This book is on a mission to save the planet. According to Yale Environment 360, "Human activities are causing an alarming decline in biodiversity that is endangering food security, clean water, energy supplies, economies, and livelihoods." Raising and marketing heirloom vegetables provides a viable solution to that problem. This book makes the case that heirlooms are vital to the planet and that heirlooms can increase a small farm's profitability.

This book details 15 reasons why heirlooms are superior to modern scientifically engineered vegetables, how to brand heirloom produce, and 22 proven heirloom marketing tips. Also, it offers marketing information, descriptions, and tips for 473 different heirloom varieties. For each heirloom profiled, this book describes its history, competitive advantage, marketing tips, sales strategies, production, companion planting, uses, and fun facts.

This information-packed marketing guide will help farmers sell more produce to more people while doing something great for the planet. This incredible resource belongs in the library of all mission-driven farms and garden enthusiasts.

This book provides the tools to grow heirlooms in the garden as well as in the market. It is a map for restoring heirloom produce to mainstream production and returning family farms to profitability.

Also available on Amazon

Farm business literature is full of memoirs offering entertaining stories with some basic cattle or produce advice but no real substance for the reader. *Big Ideas, Small Farm* is not another feel-good farm memoir devoid of authentic information, hope, or insights. This book is different; it is about results.

Big Ideas, Small Farm is about growing small farm profitability. This book is part self-help and part marketing strategies because marketing tips and theories are helpful when the people implementing them believe in them. Small farm marketing is a mindset as much as it is a practice. This mindset requires believing big ideas create big results. Effective marketing turns small farms into sustainable businesses.

Big Ideas, Small Farm is for the people who want to grow small farms into highly profitable businesses. This book includes 39 broad strategies broken down into 376 best practices that will turn any farm dream into a business reality.

Too many farm business books are written by farming aristocrats: people who inherited their success. There is nothing wrong with inheriting a farm, but building a farm business from scratch requires different skills, expertise, and ways of thinking than inheriting a farm.